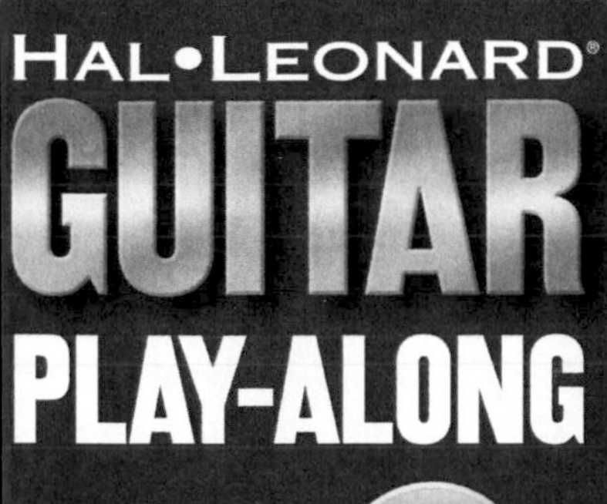

BLUES

T0058874

AUDIO ACCESS INCLUDED

To access audio visit:
www.halleonard.com/mylibrary

Enter Code
7231-8095-1256-9647

Tracking, mixing, and mastering by Jake Johnson
All guitars by Doug Boduch
Bass by Tom McGirr
Keyboards by Warren Wiegratz
Drums by Scott Schroedl

ISBN 978-0-634-05627-7

Visit Hal Leonard Online at www.halleonard.com

HAL•LEONARD®
7777 W. BLUEMOUND RD. P.O. BOX 13819

HAL•LEONARD®

GUITAR PLAY-ALONG

AUDIO ACCESS INCLUDED

BLUES

All Your Love
(I Miss Loving)

Words and Music by Otis Rush

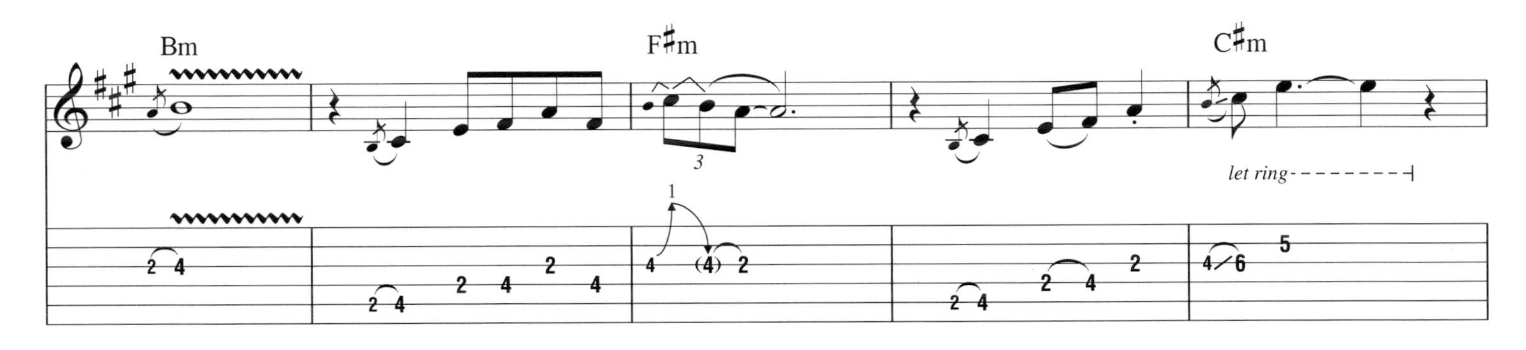

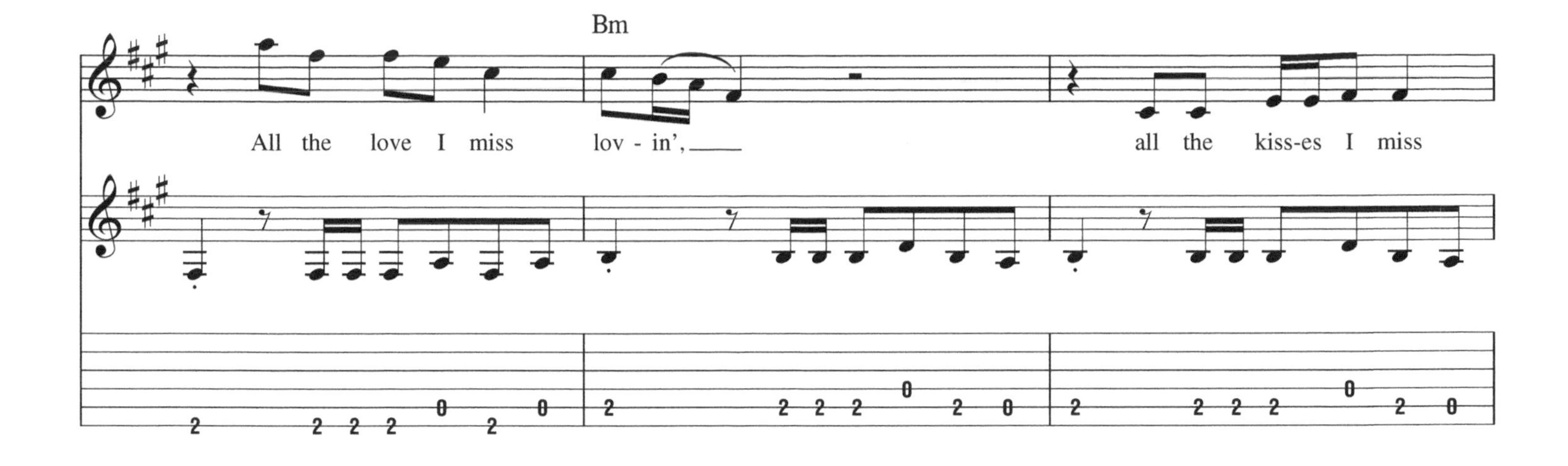
Bm
All the love I miss lov - in',
all the kiss-es I miss

F♯m
C♯m
kiss - in'.
Be - fore I met you, ba - by,

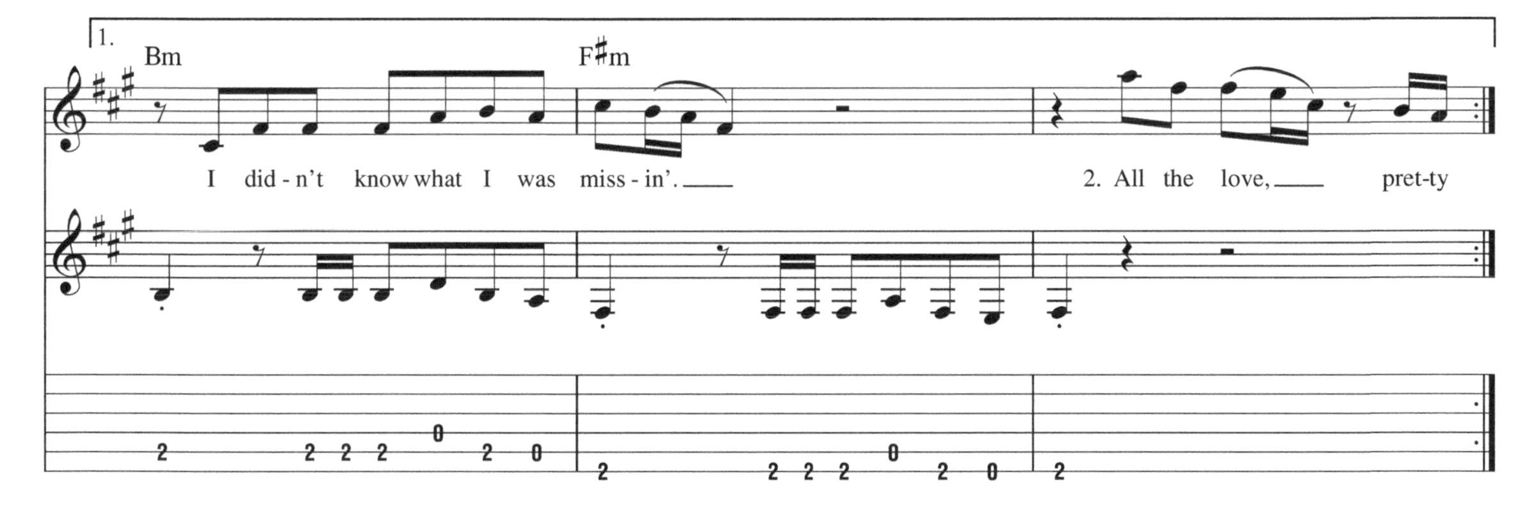
1.
Bm
F♯m
I did - n't know what I was miss - in'.
2. All the love, pret-ty

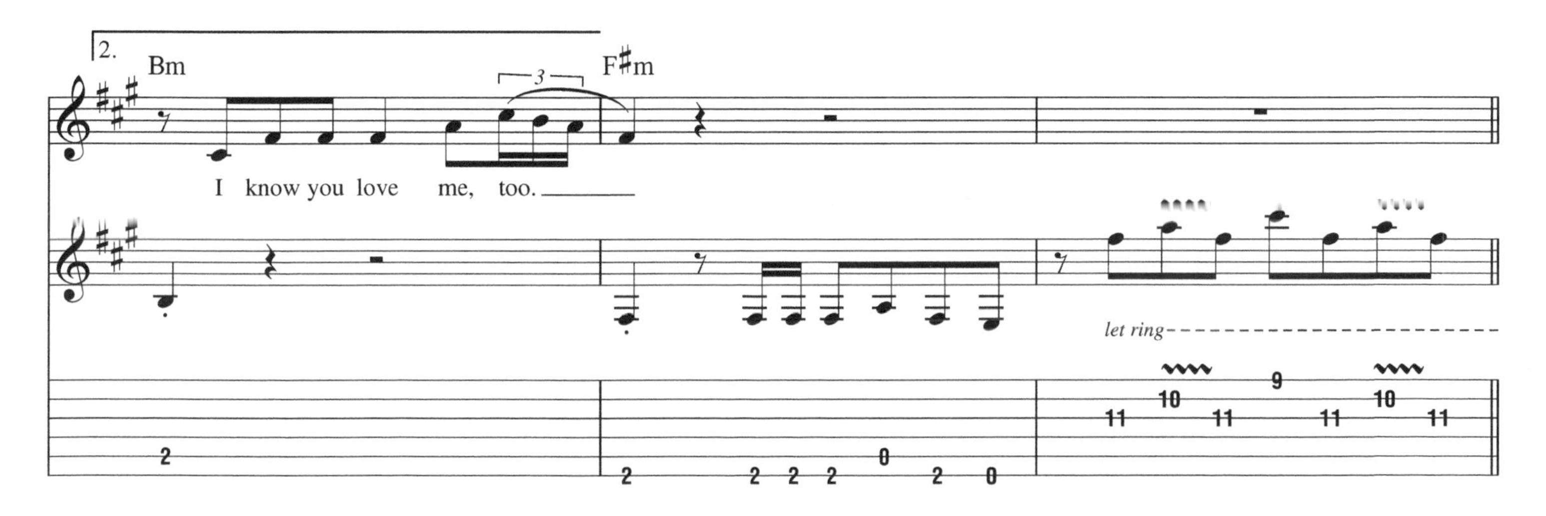
2.
Bm
F♯m
I know you love me, too.
let ring

Interlude

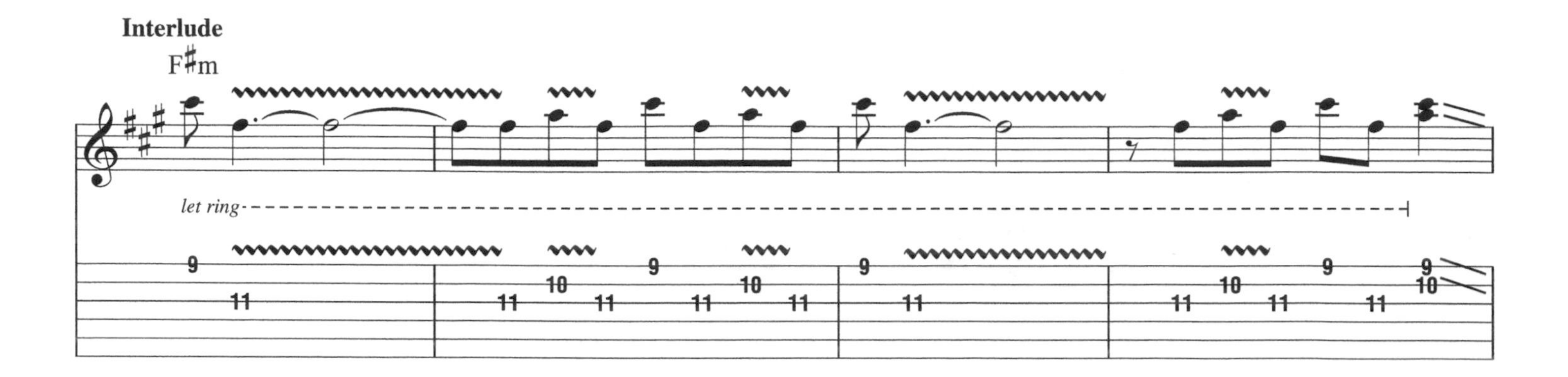

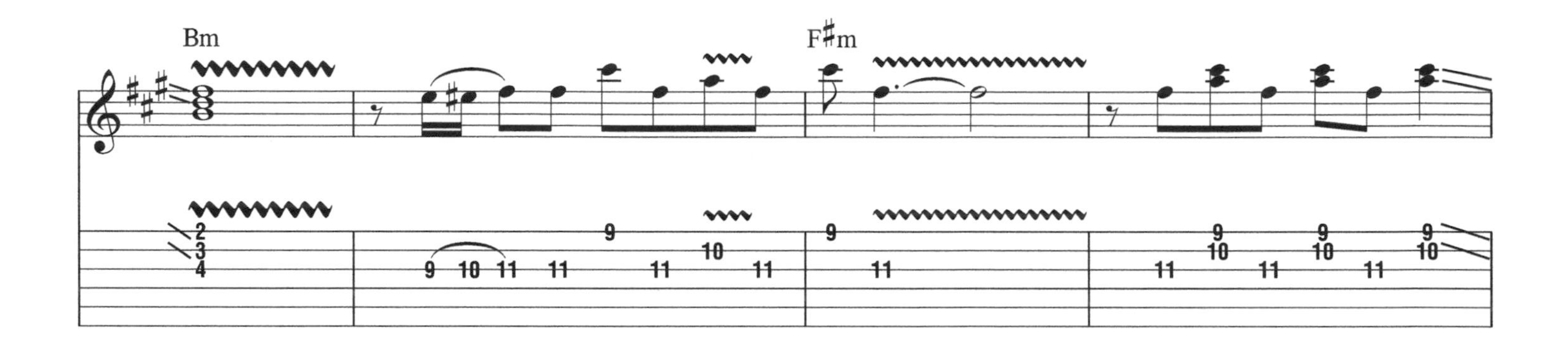

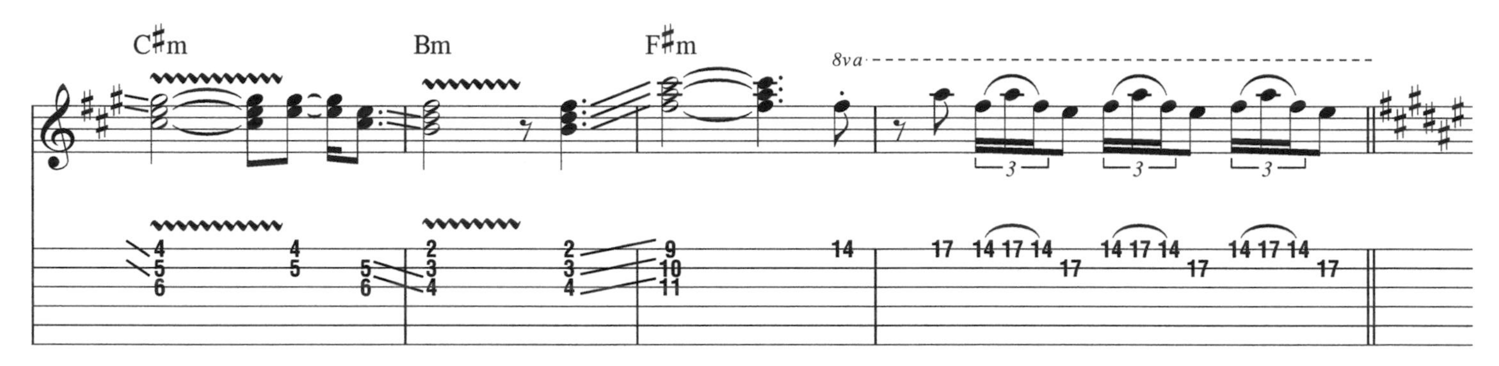

Guitar Solo

F♯7

8va

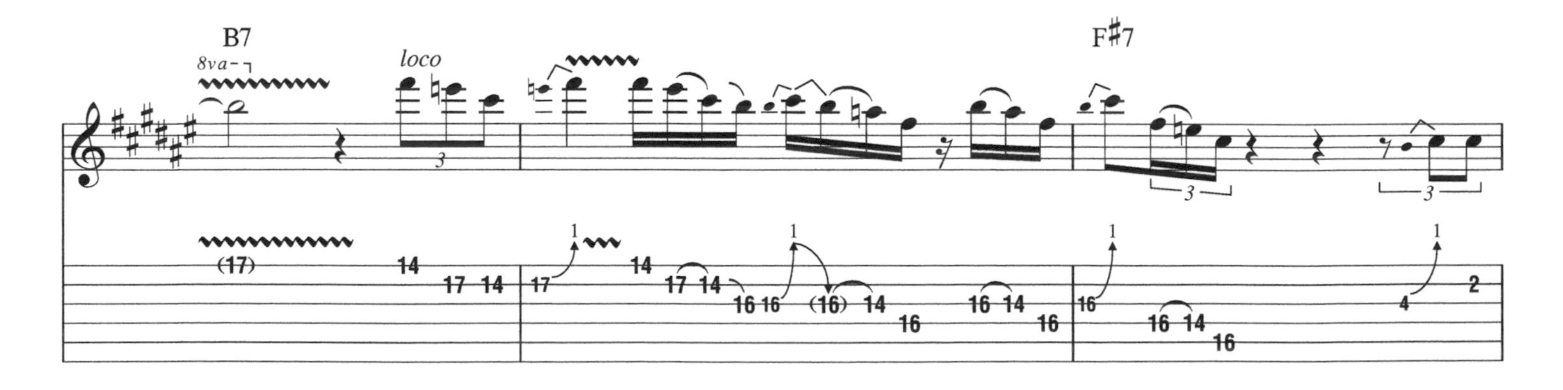

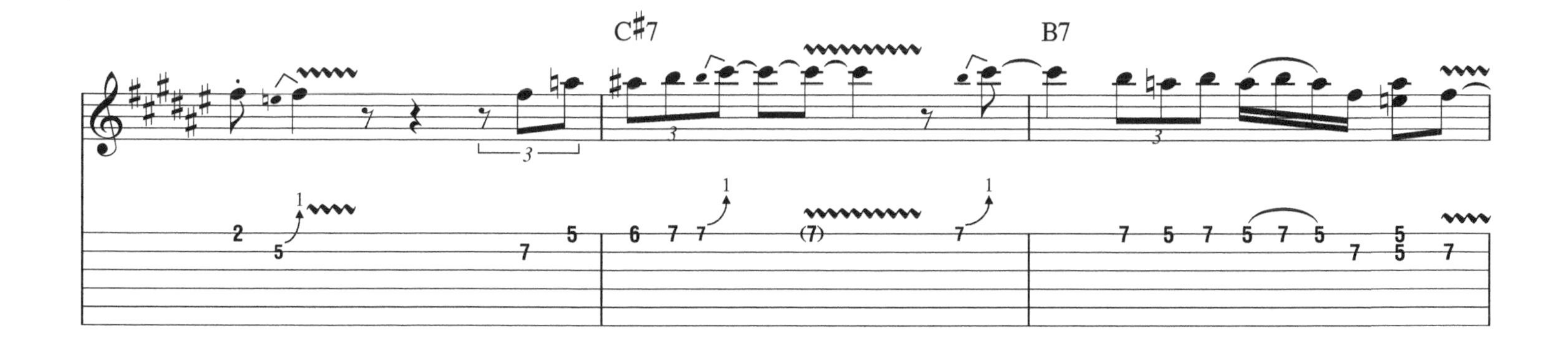
C♯7
B7
2 5 1 7 5
6 7 7 1 (7) 7 1
7 5 7 5 7 5 7 5 5 7

F♯7
Chorus
F♯7
Whoa, whoa, whoa, ba - by.
(7) 7 5 6 6 6 7 6 7 6 7 6
7 1
2 2 4 6 6 4 4 7 4

You know I love you, ba - by.
Yeah,
4 4 6 6 4 4 6 4
2 2 4 6 6 4 4 7 7
4 4 7 7 4 6 2 4

B7
F♯7
yeah, ba - by.
You know I love you, ba - by.
2 2 4 6 6 4 4 6 4
7 7 6 4 4 6 4
2 2 4 6 6 4 4 6 6

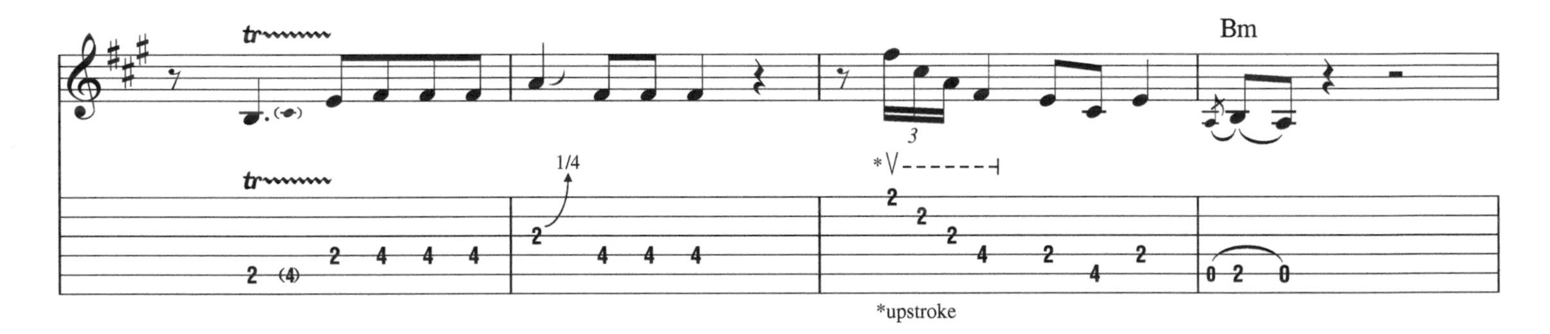

Additional Lyrics

2. All the love, pretty baby,
   I have in store for you.
   All the love, pretty baby,
   I have in store for you.
   The way I love you, baby,
   I know you love me, too.

Born Under a Bad Sign

Words and Music by Booker T. Jones and William Bell

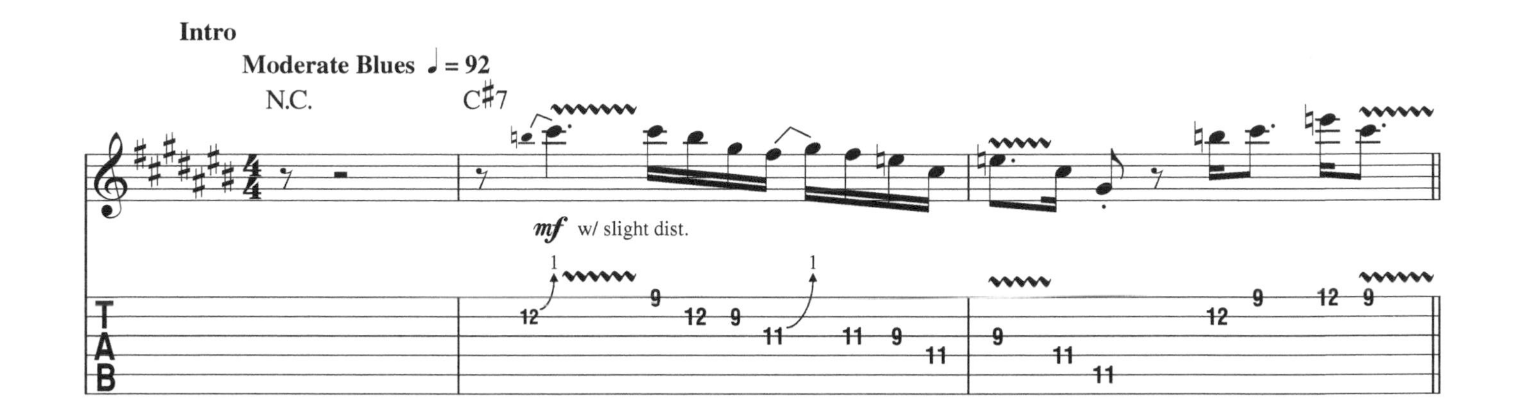

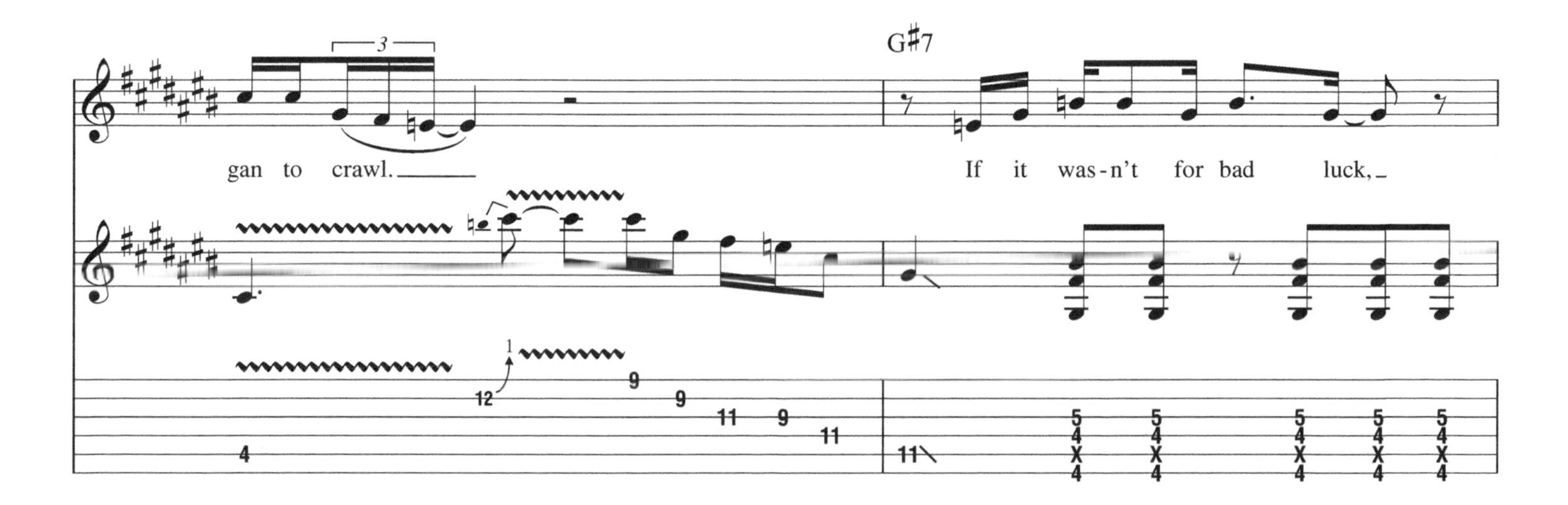

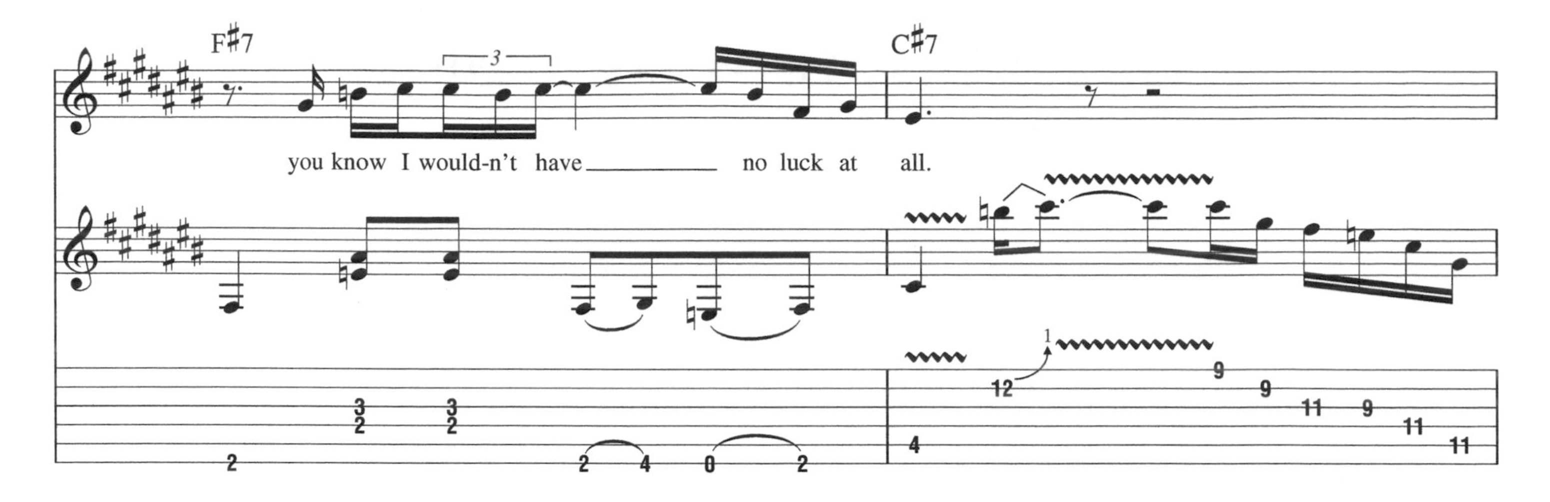
F♯7
C♯7
you know I would-n't have no luck at all.

Verse
C♯7
1. Hard luck and trou-ble been my on - ly friend.

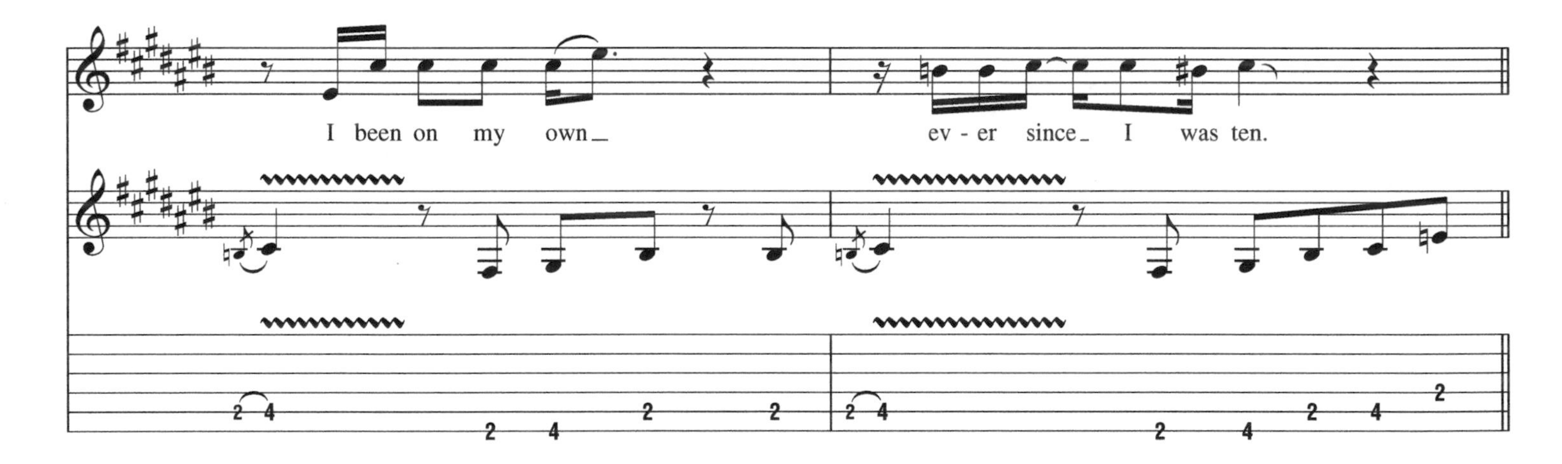
I been on my own ev - er since I was ten.

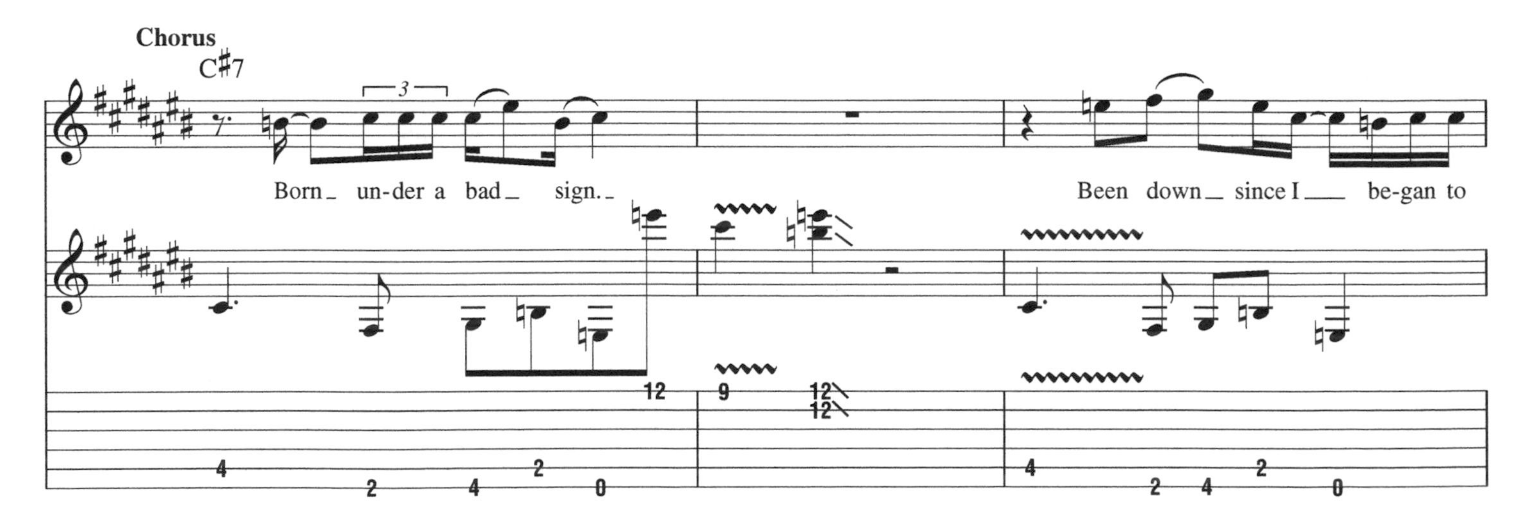
Chorus
C♯7
Born un-der a bad sign. Been down since I be-gan to

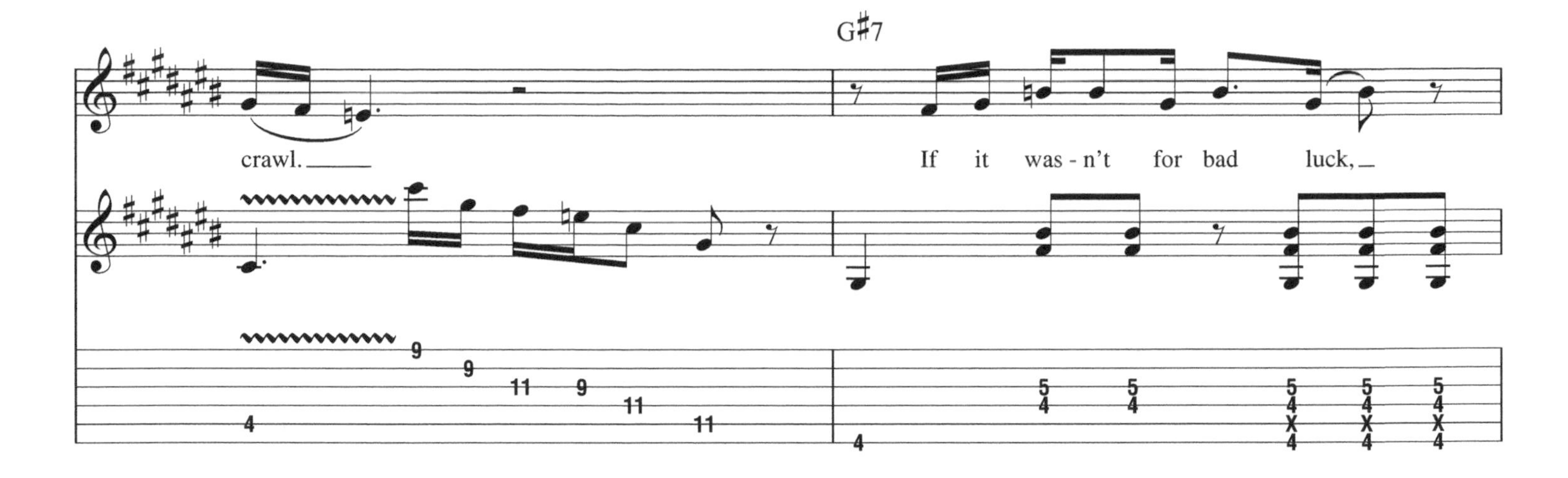
G♯7
crawl.
If it was-n't for bad luck,

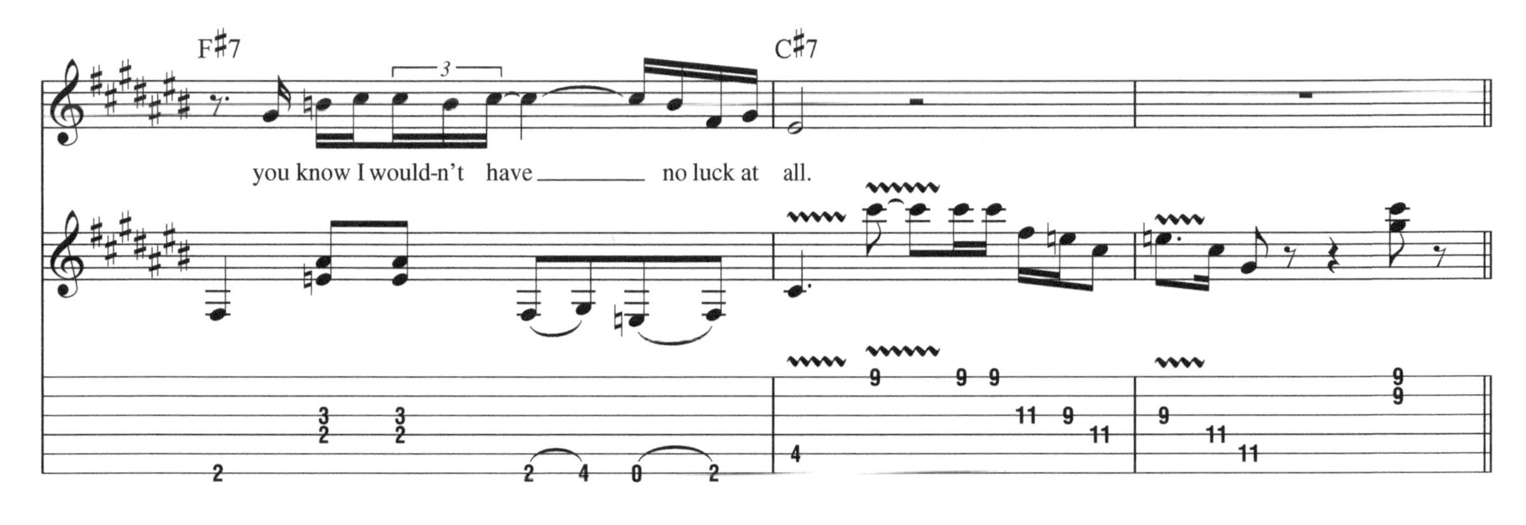
F♯7
C♯7
you know I would-n't have no luck at all.

Verse
C♯7
2. I can't read,
3. See additional lyrics
I did-n't learn how to write.

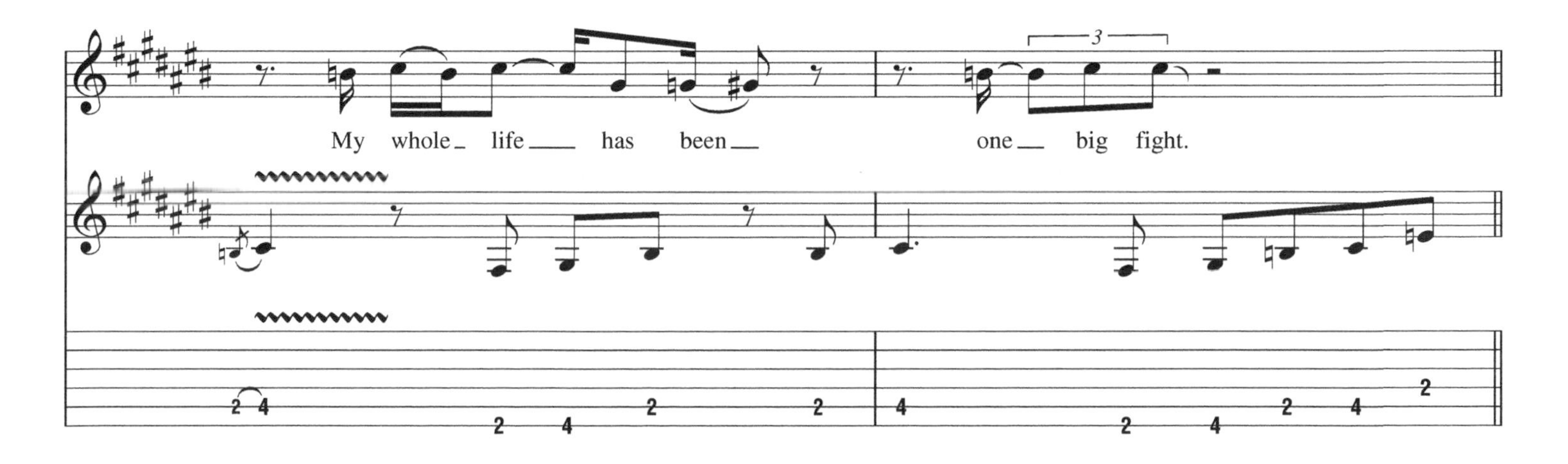
My whole life has been one big fight.

Chorus
C#7
Born un - der a bad sign.
I been down since I be - gan to crawl.
To Coda
G#7
F#7
If it was - n't for bad luck,
I say, I would - n't have no luck
C#7
at all,
Spoken: 'n' that ain't no lie.
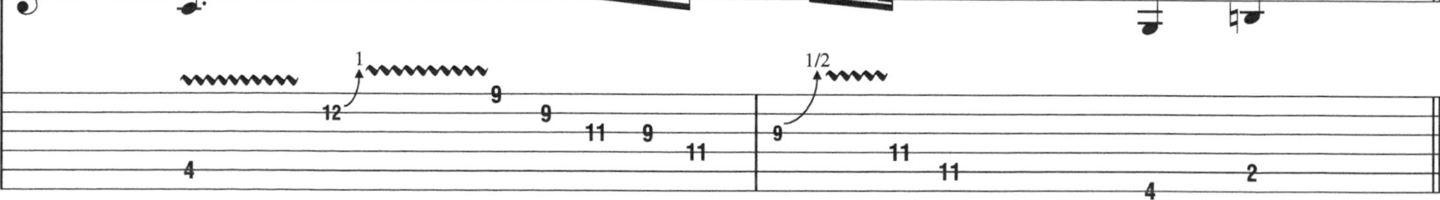

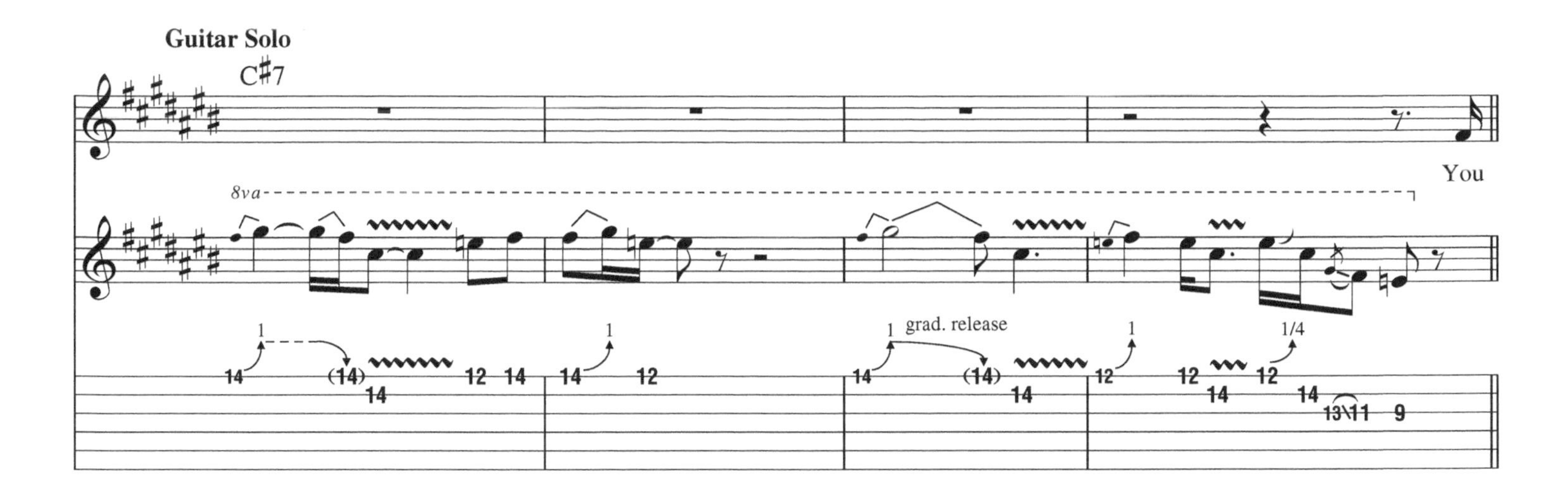
Guitar Solo
C♯7
You
8va
grad. release
1/4

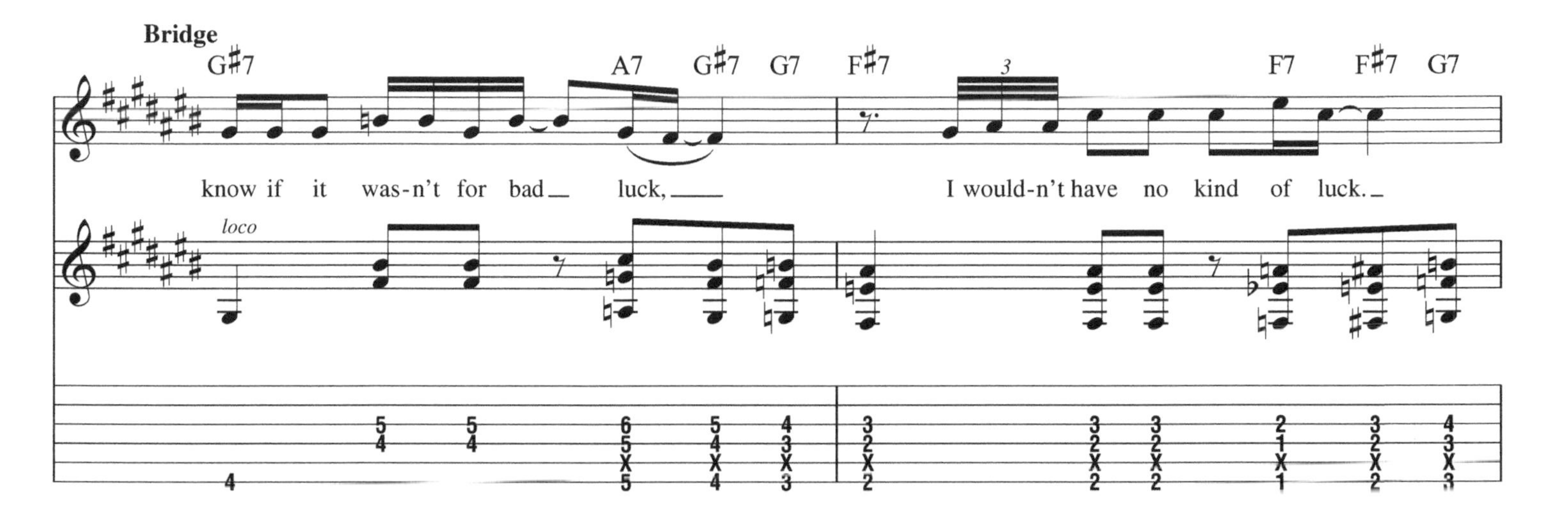
Bridge
G♯7
A7 G♯7 G7
F♯7
F7 F♯7 G7
know if it was-n't for bad luck,
I would-n't have no kind of luck.
loco

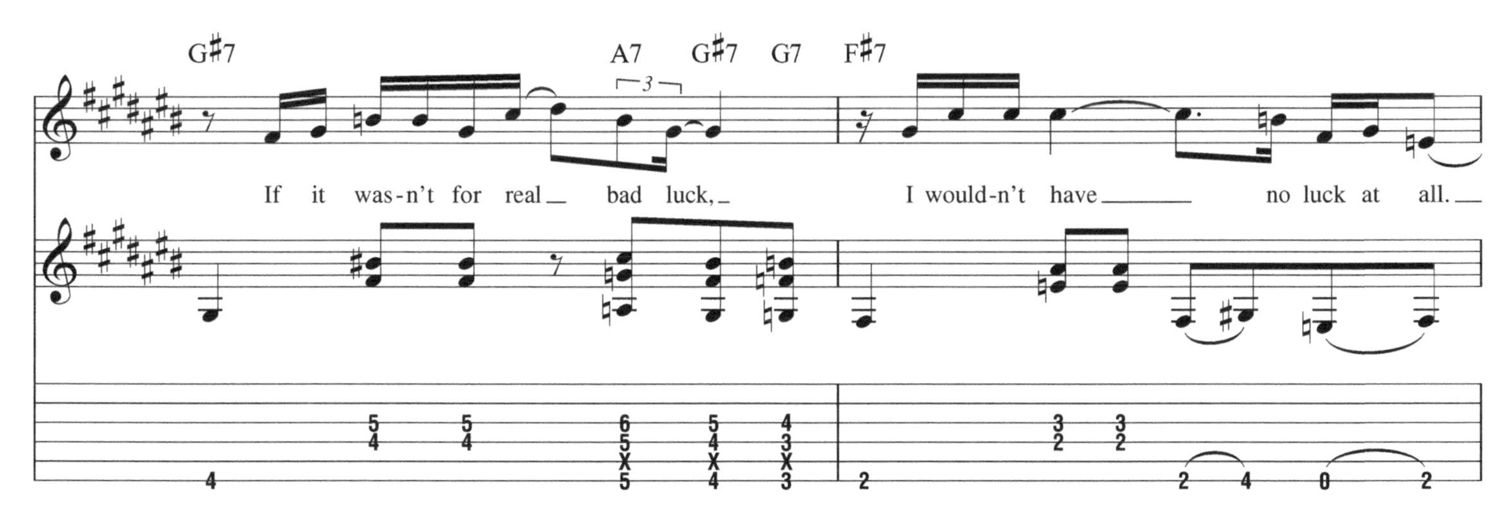
G♯7
A7 G♯7 G7
F♯7
If it was-n't for real bad luck,
I would-n't have no luck at all.

C♯7
D.S. al Coda
1/2

Additional Lyrics

3. You know wine and women
Is all I crave.
A big leg woman gonna carry me
To my grave.

Hide Away

By Freddie King and Sonny Thompson

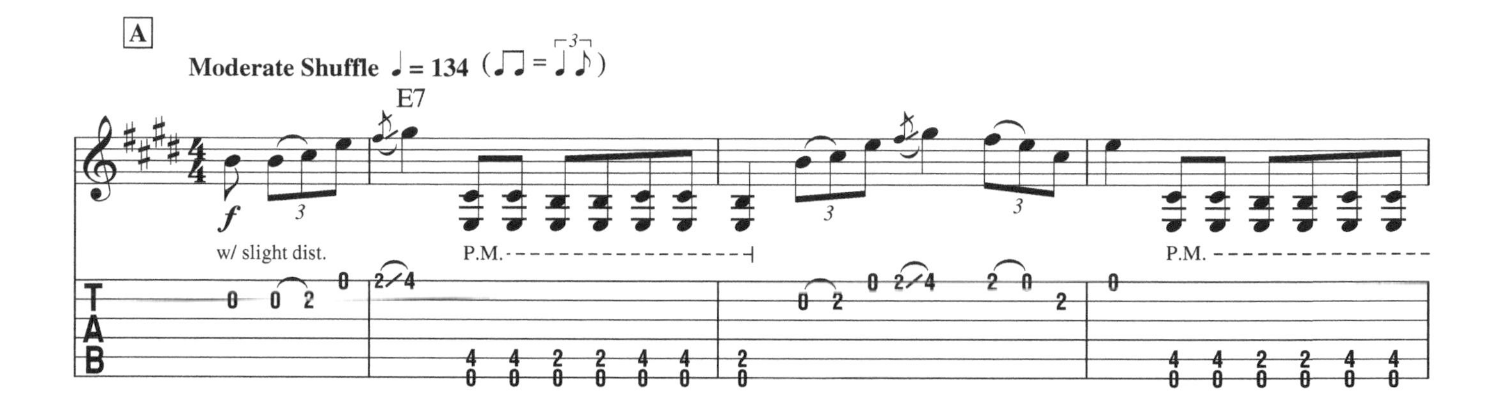

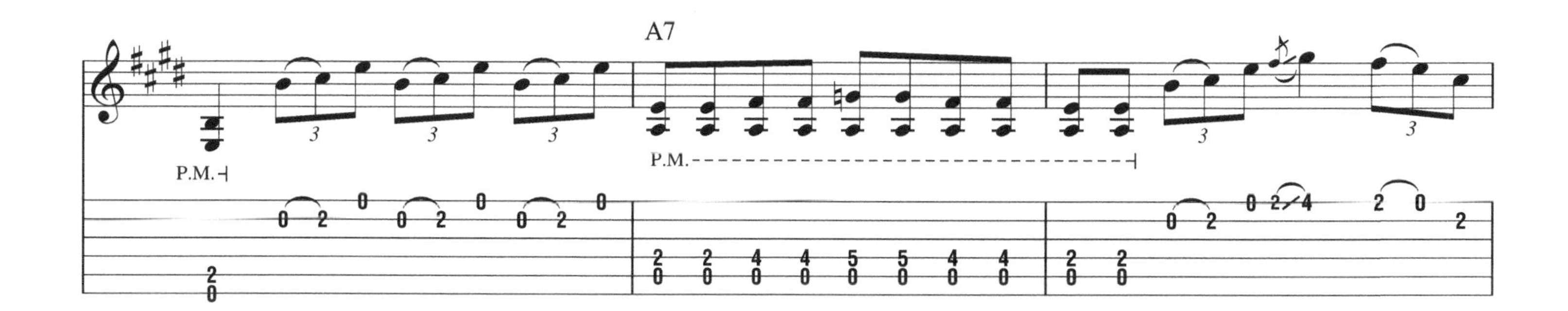

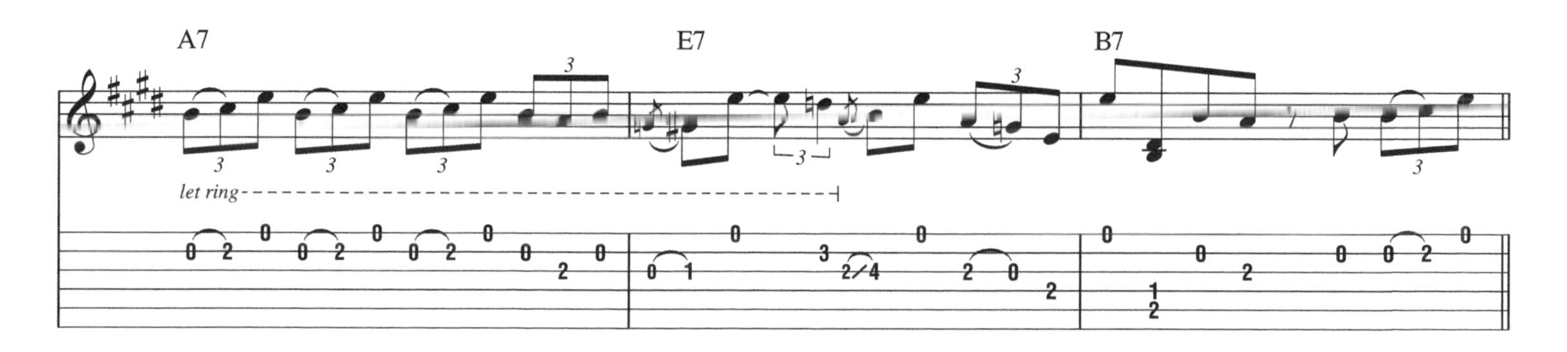

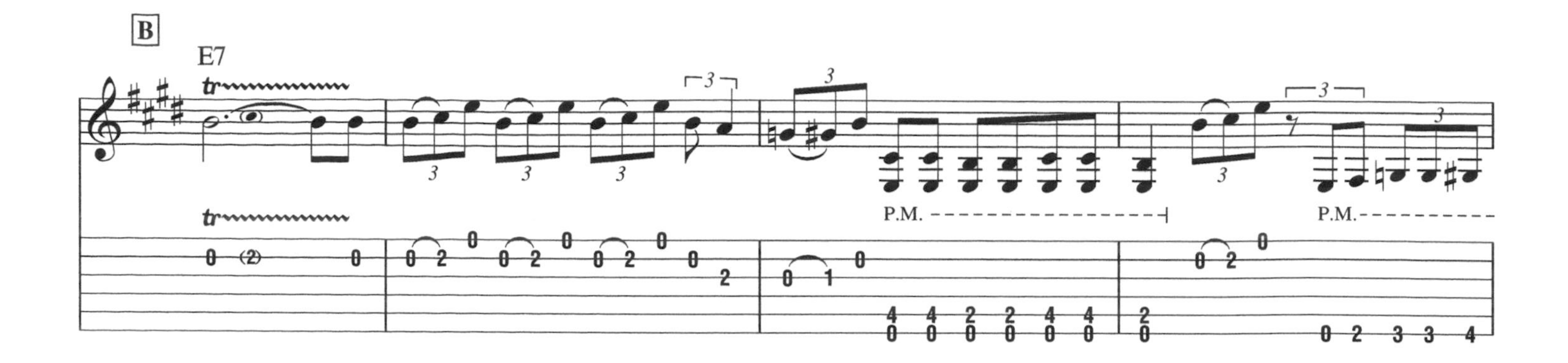
B
E7
tr
P.M.
P.M.

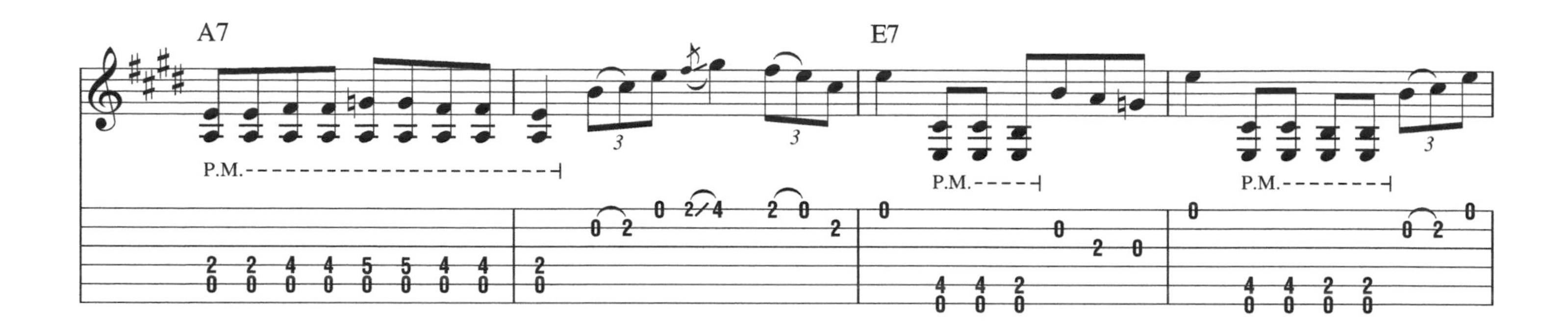
A7
E7
P.M.
P.M.
P.M.

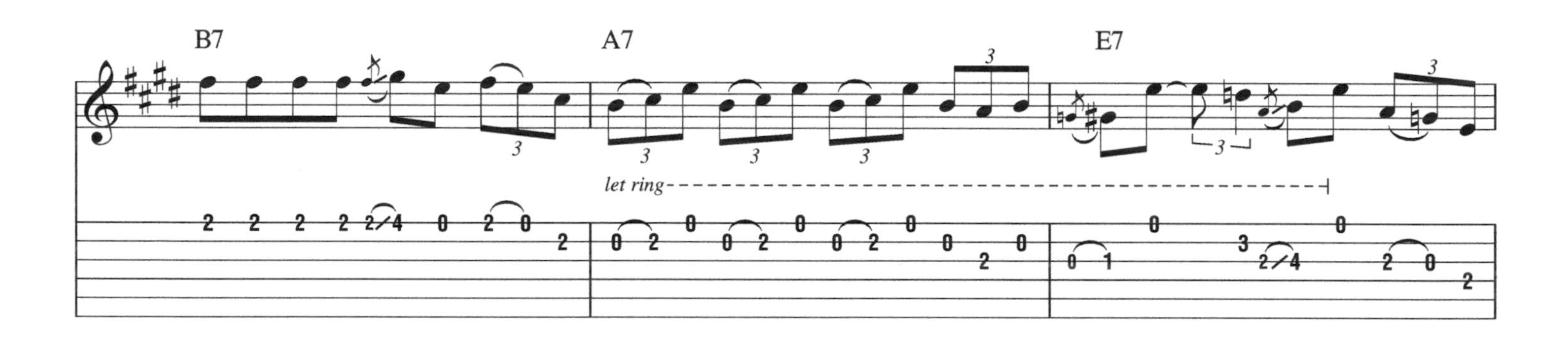
B7
A7
E7
let ring

C
B7
E7

A7
E7
P.M.

B7
E7
tr

D
E7
P.M.

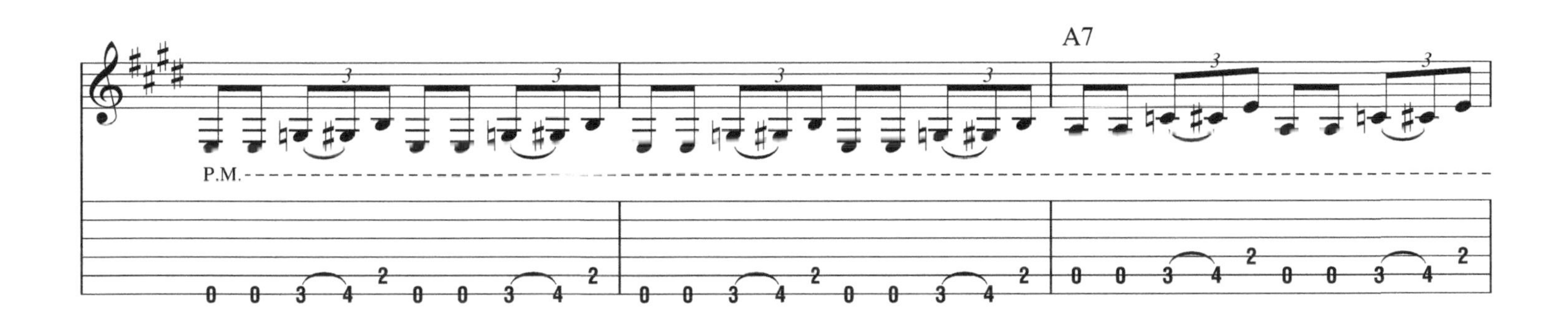
A7
P.M.

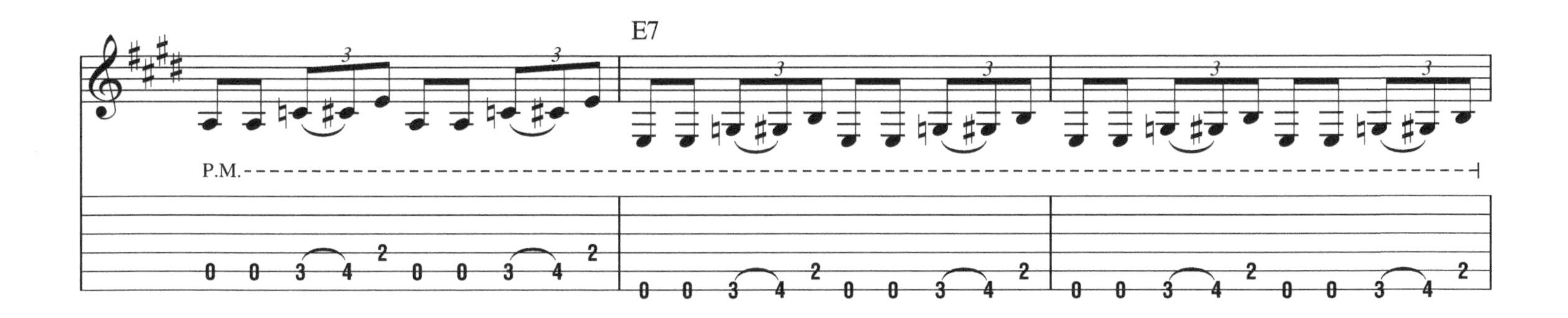
E7
P.M.

B7
A7
B7

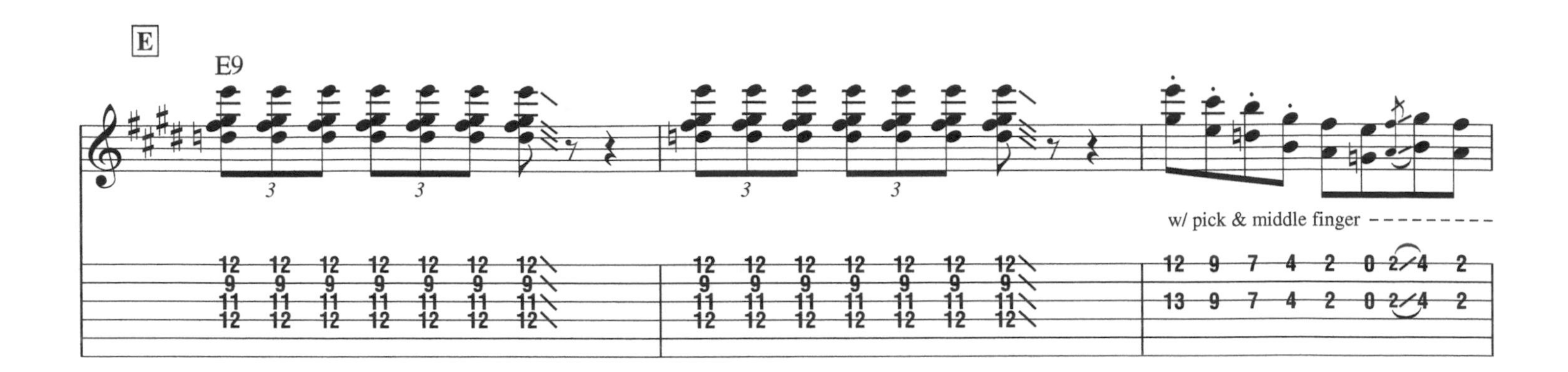
E
E9
w/ pick & middle finger

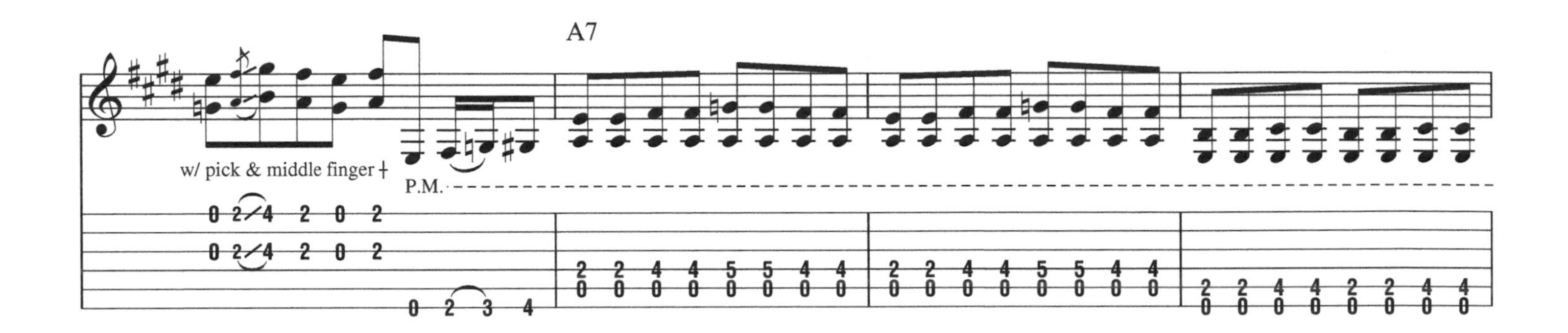
A7
w/ pick & middle finger
P.M.

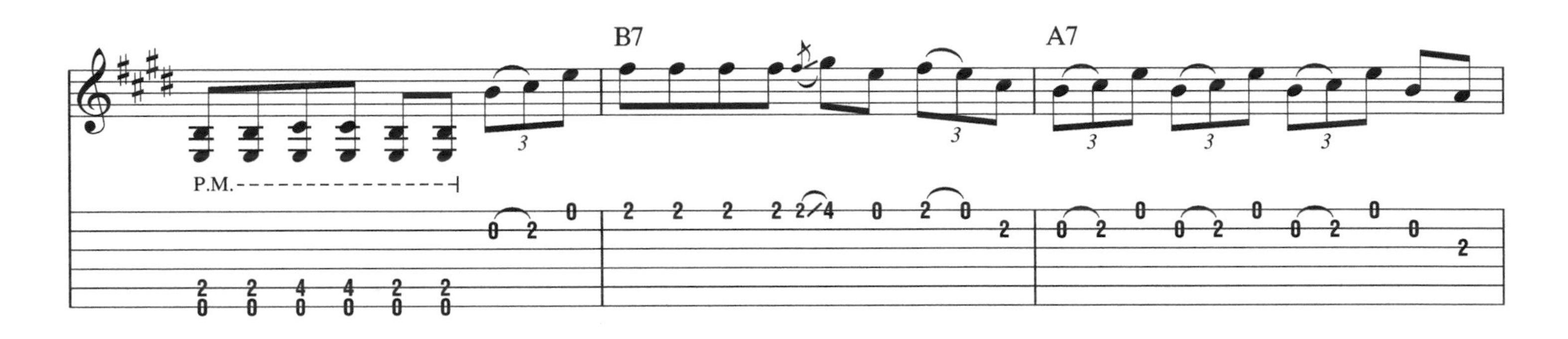
B7
A7
P.M.

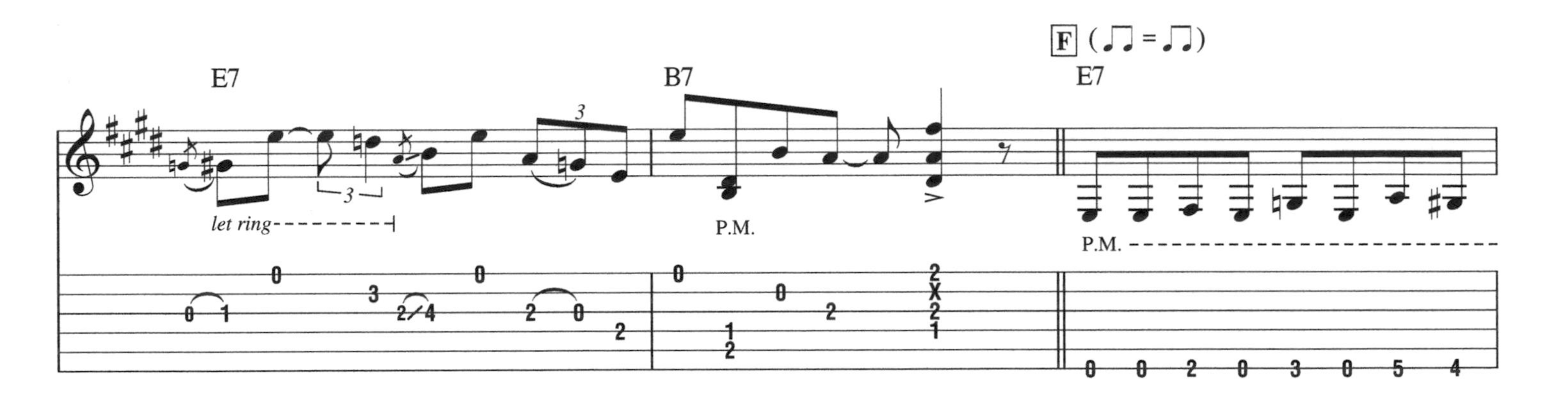
E7
B7
F
E7
let ring
P.M.

A7
P.M.

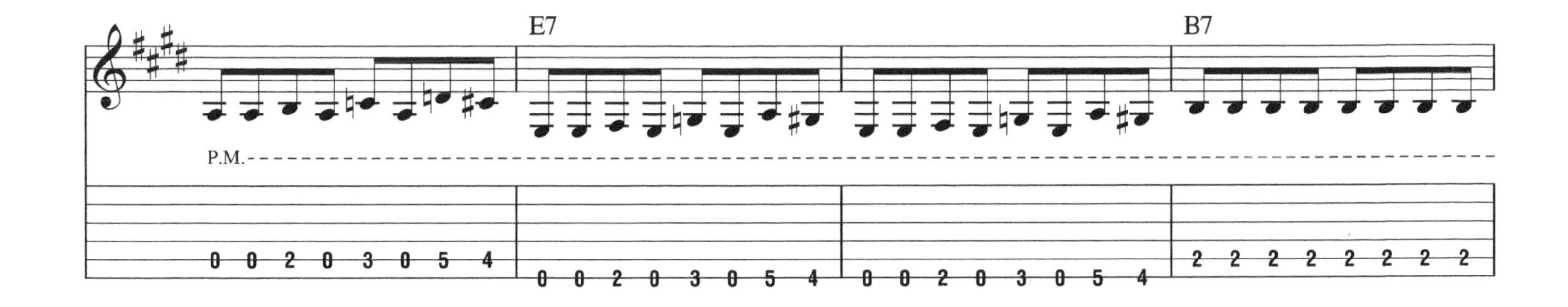
E7
B7
P.M.

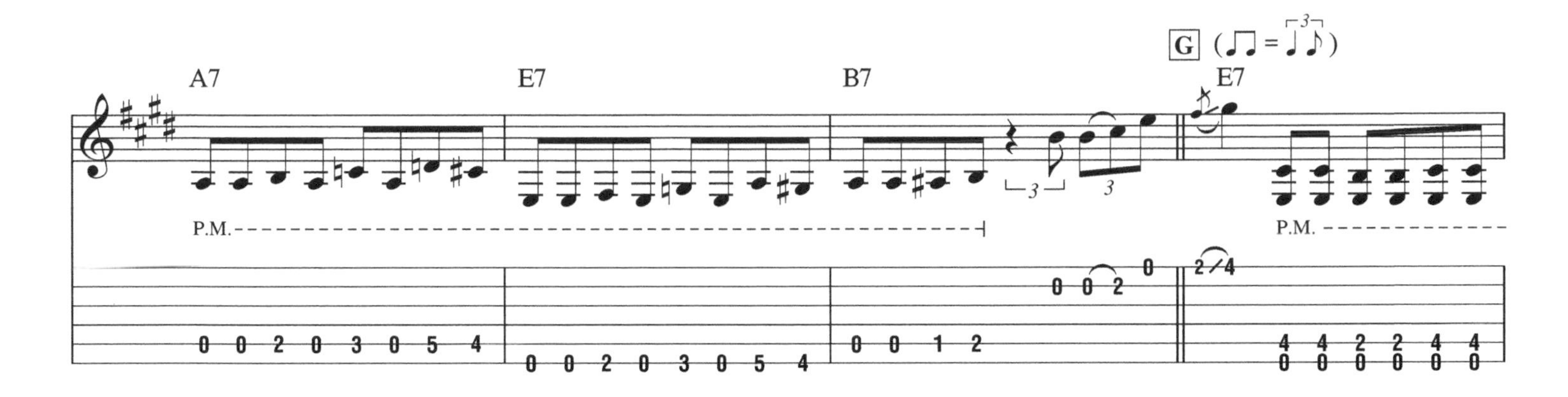
A7
E7
B7
G
E7
P.M.
P.M.

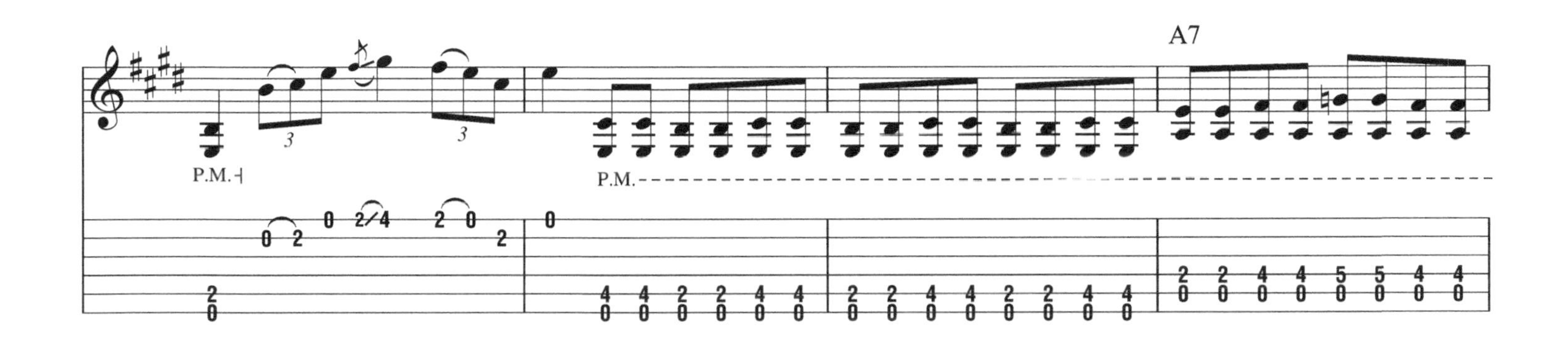
A7
P.M.
P.M.

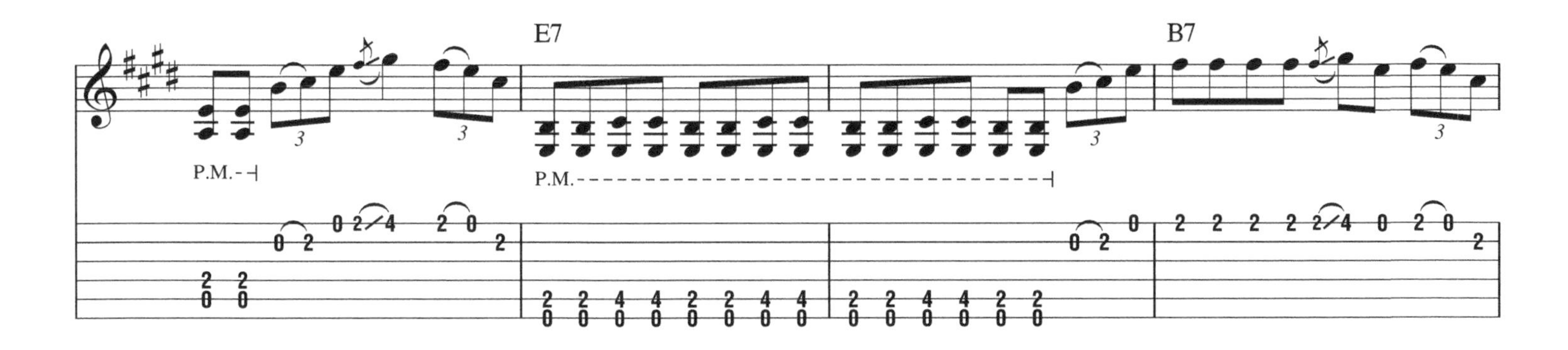
E7
B7
P.M.
P.M.

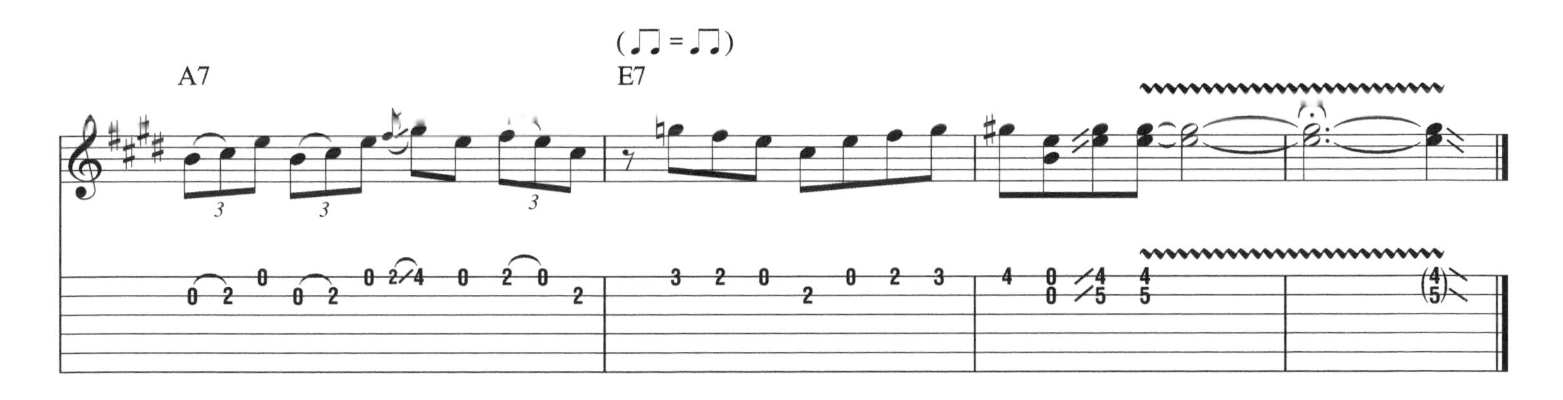
A7
E7

I'm Tore Down

Words and Music by Sonny Thompson

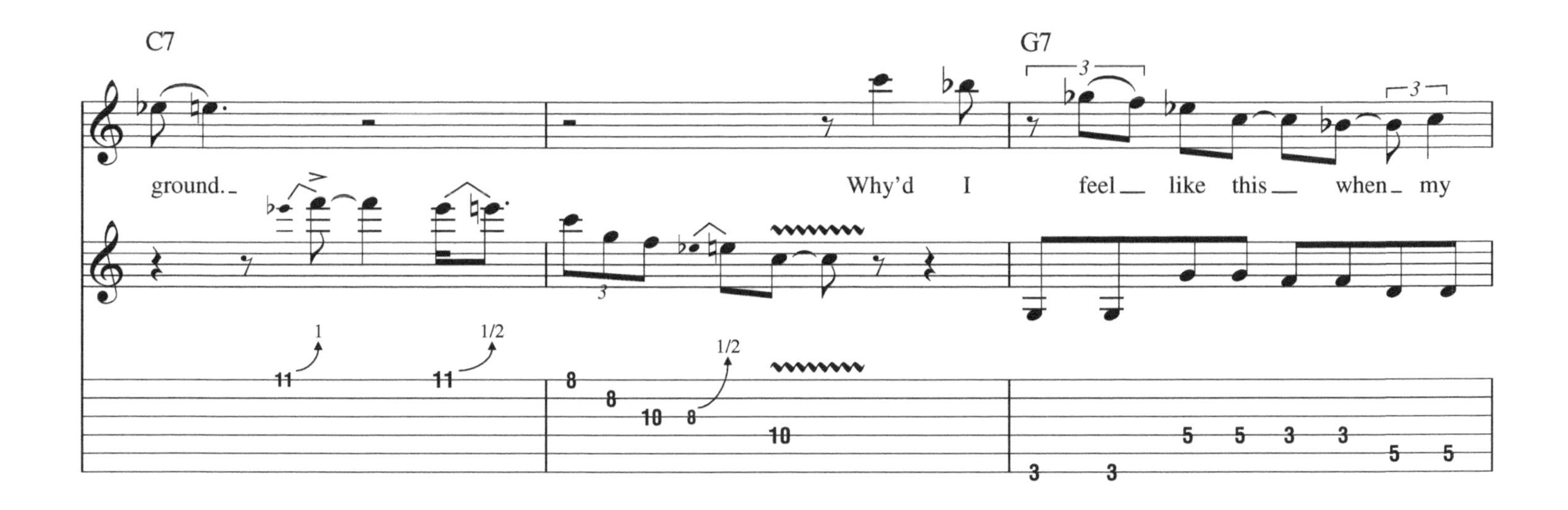
C7
G7
ground.
Why'd I
feel like this when my

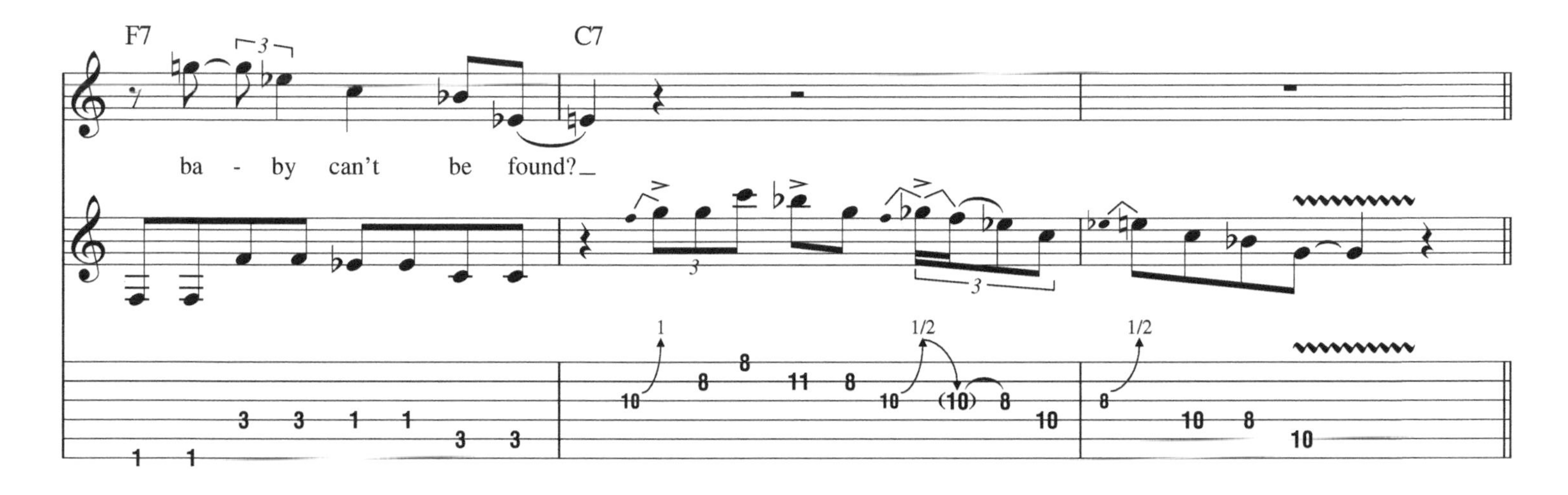
F7
C7
ba - by can't be found?

Verse
C7 N.C.
F
C7 N.C.
1. Went to the riv - er, to jump in. My ba - by showed up and said,

Chorus
F7
"I will tell you when." Well, I'm tore down, al - most lev - el with the

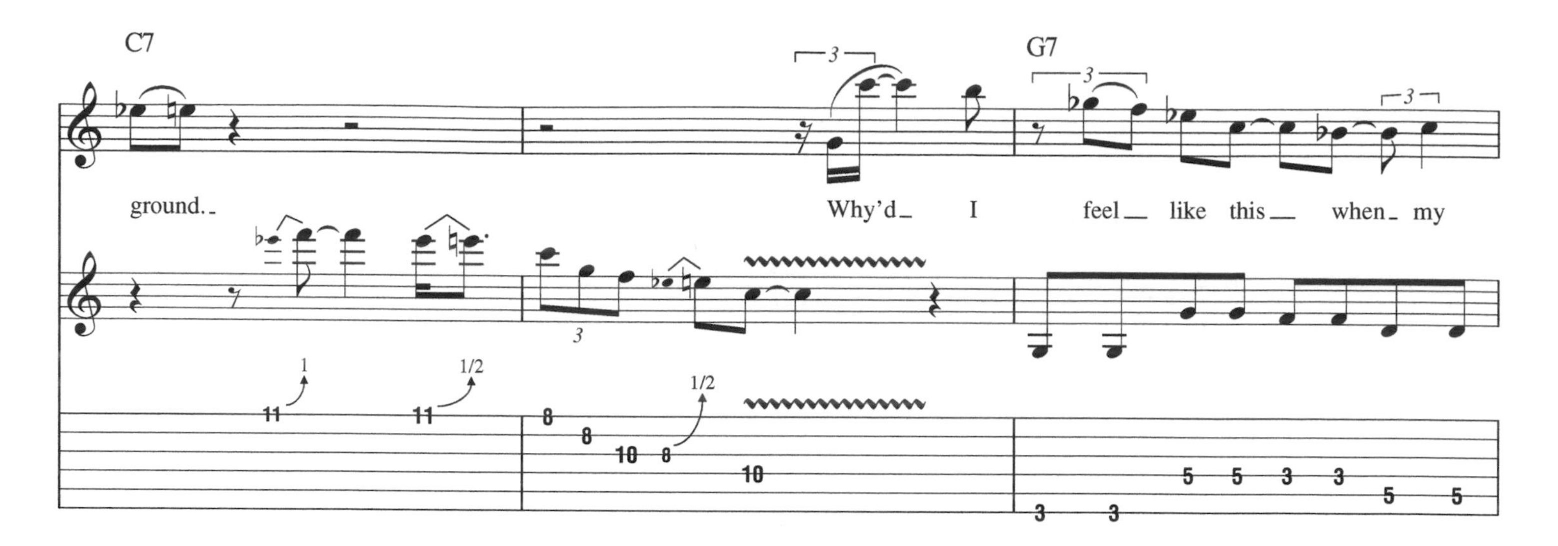
C7
G7
ground.
Why'd I feel like this when my
1
1/2
1/2

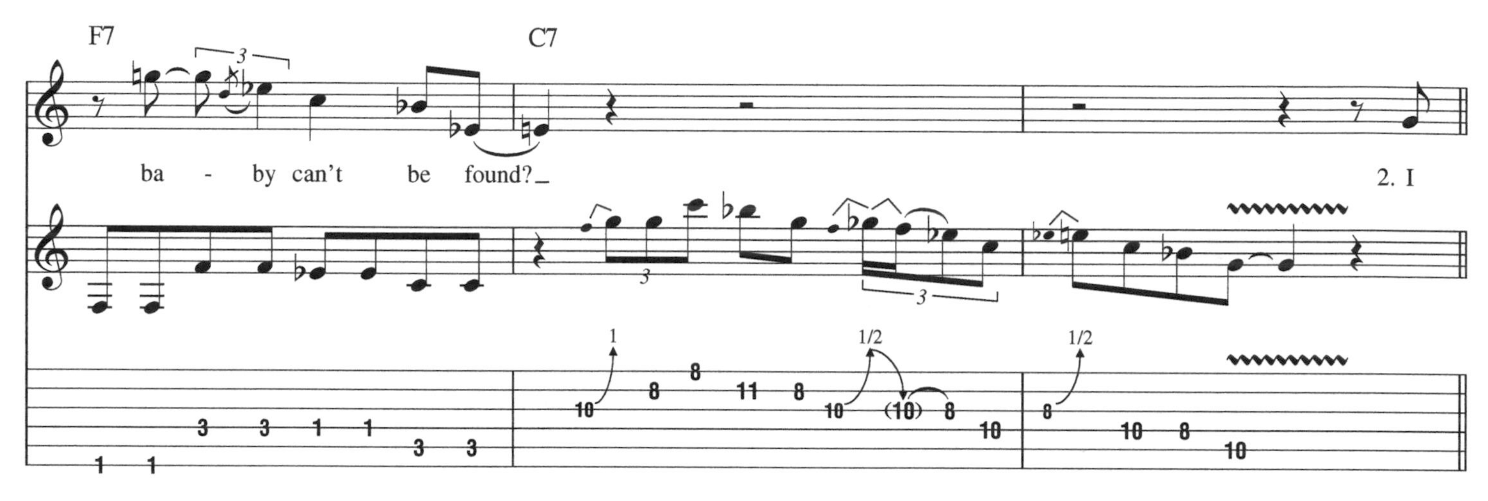
F7
C7
ba - by can't be found?
2. I
1
1/2
1/2

Verse
C7
D♭7
C7
love you, babe, with all my heart and soul. Love like mine will
3. See additional lyrics
let ring

D♭7
C7
C°7
nev - er grow old. Love you in the morn-ing and in the eve - ning too.
let ring

Chorus
C
N.C.
F7
Ev - 'ry time you leave me I get mad with you. Well, I'm tore down. I'm

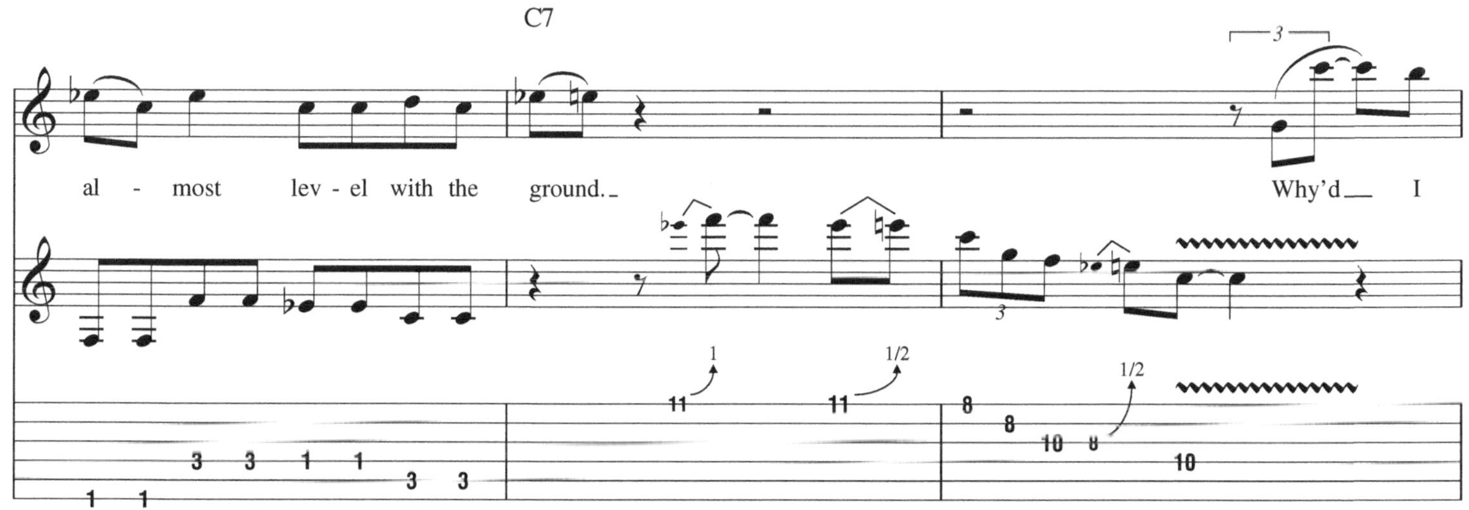
C7
al - most lev - el with the ground. Why'd I

To Coda

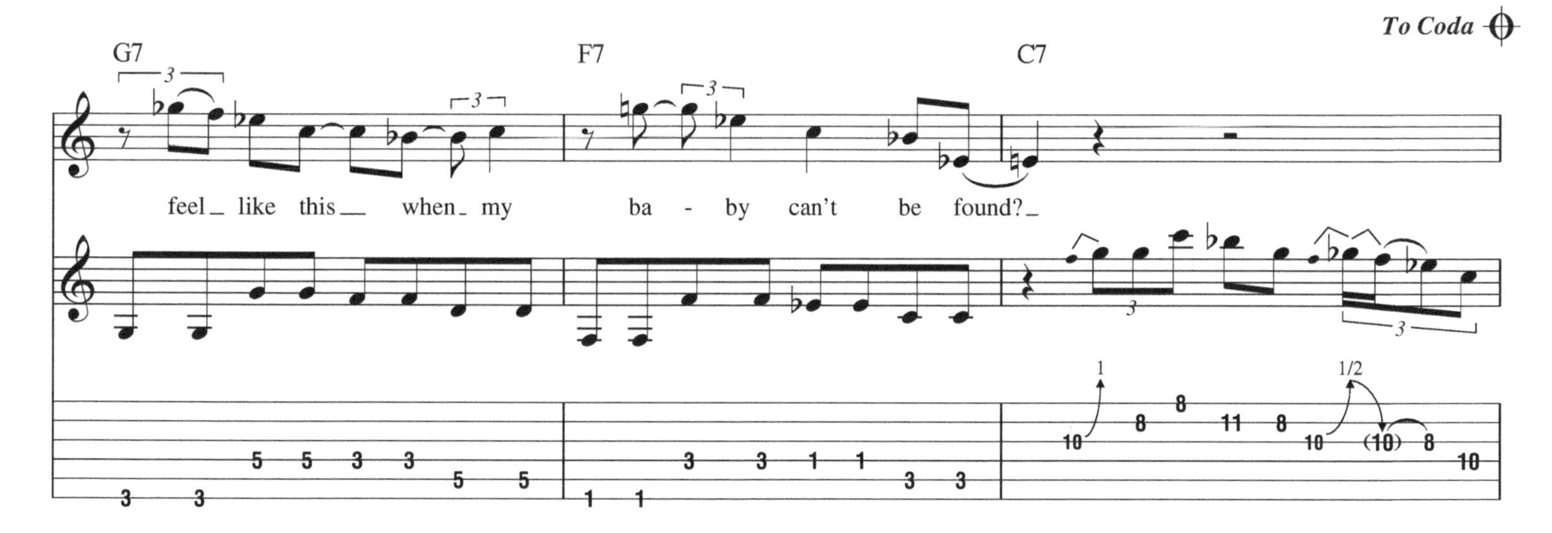
G7
F7
C7
feel like this when my ba - by can't be found?

Guitar Solo
C7

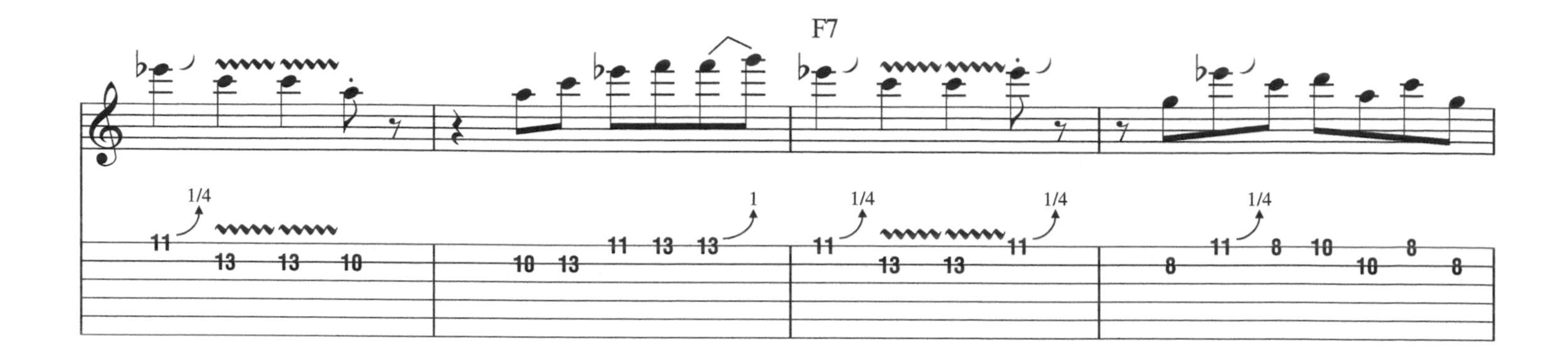
F7

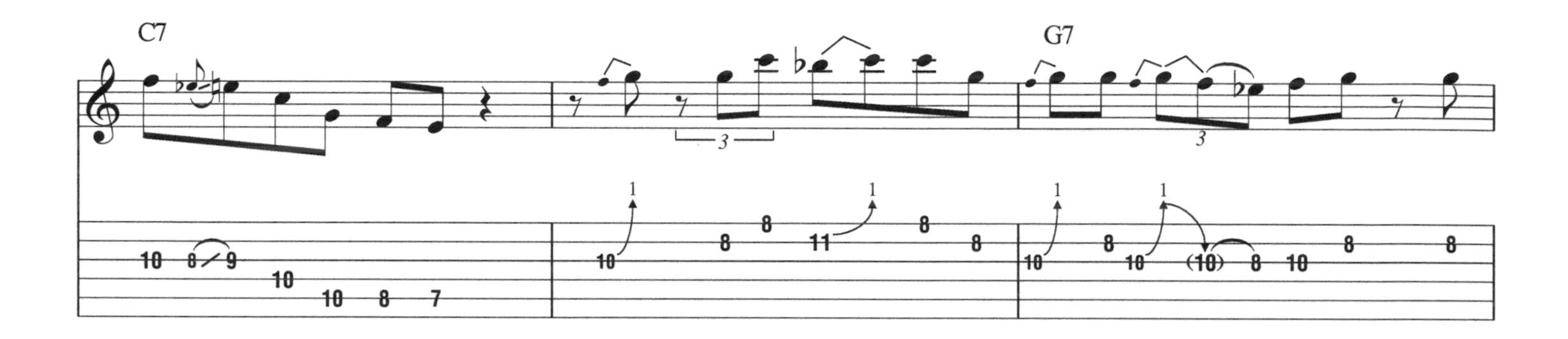
C7
G7

F7
C7

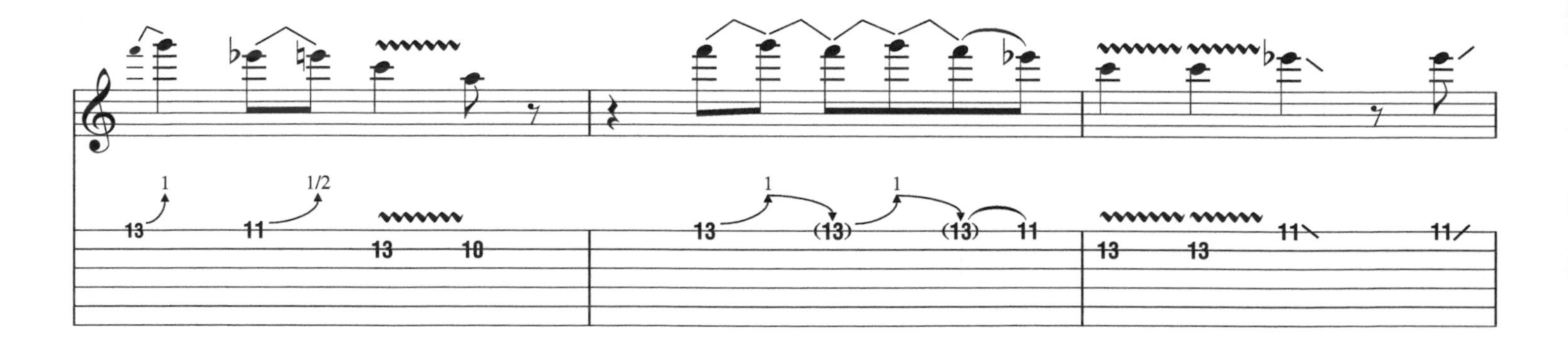

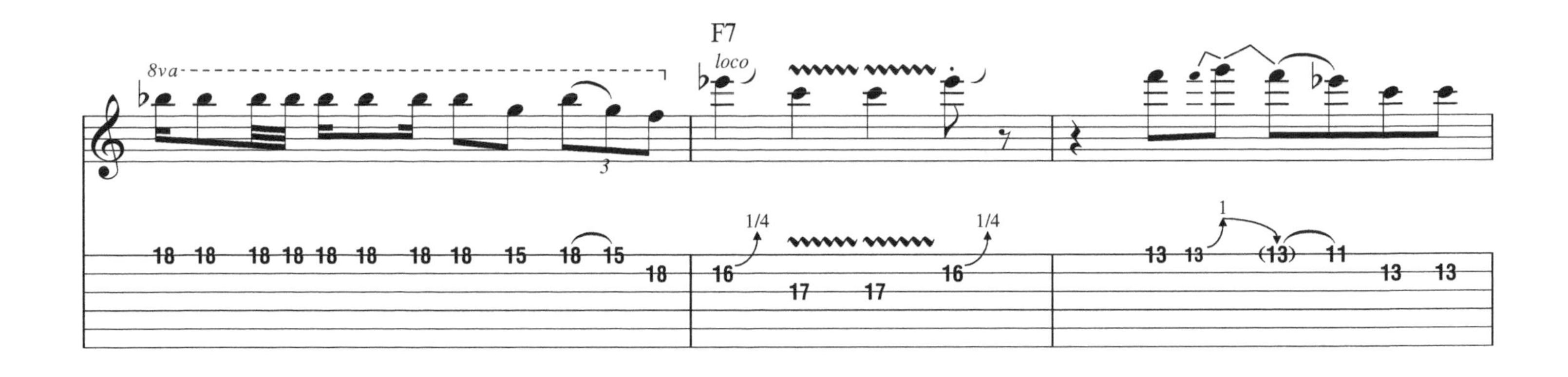
8va
F7
loco

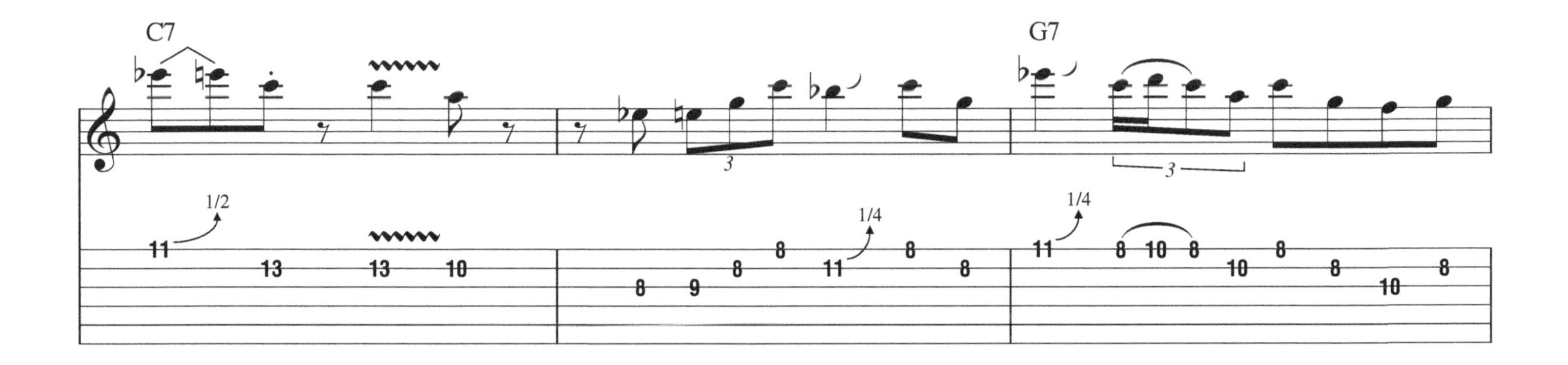
C7
G7

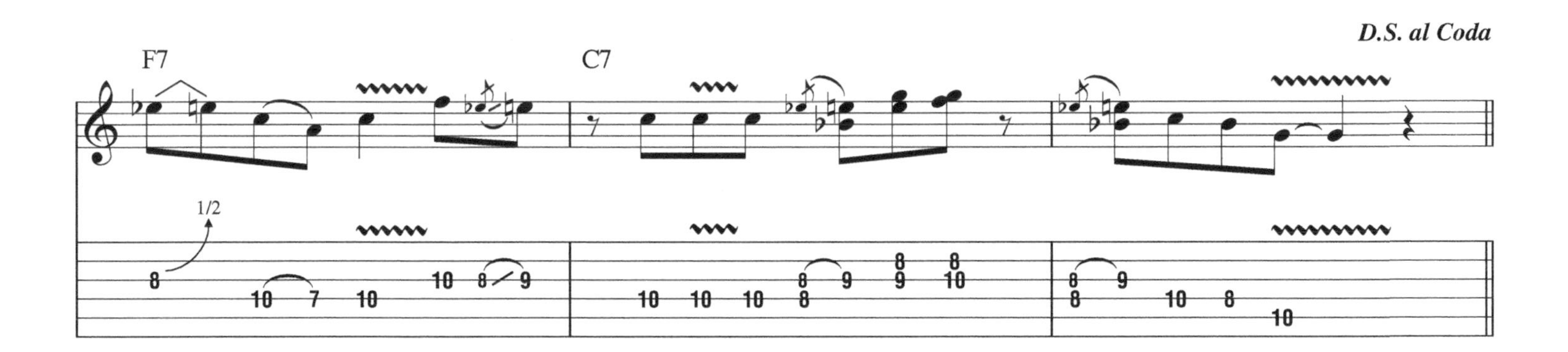
D.S. al Coda
F7
C7

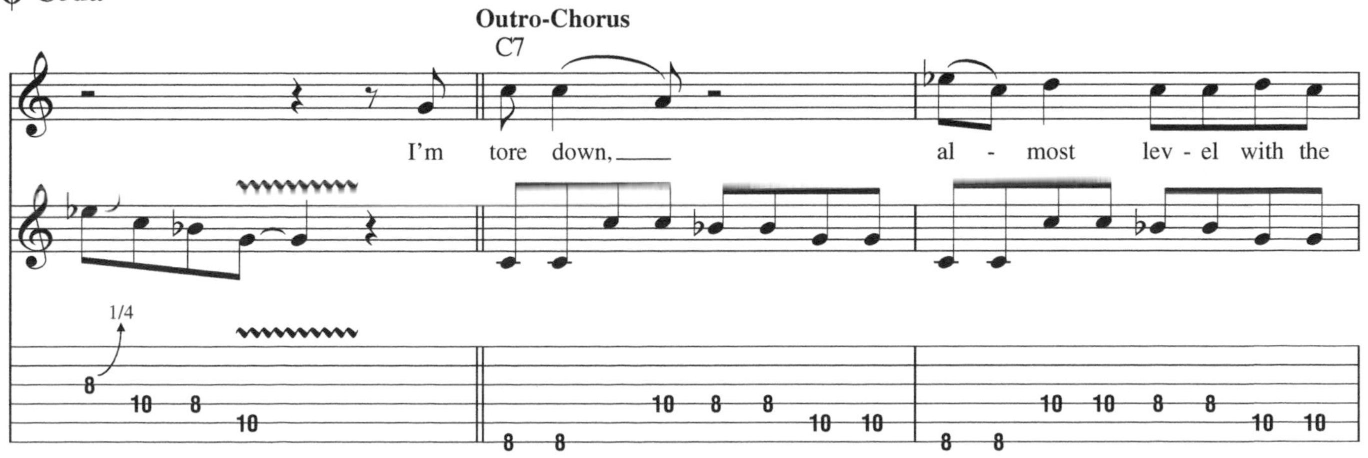
Coda
Outro-Chorus
C7
I'm tore down,
al - most lev - el with the

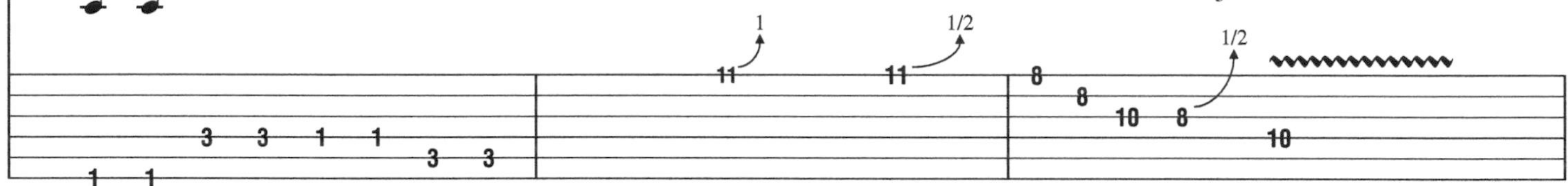

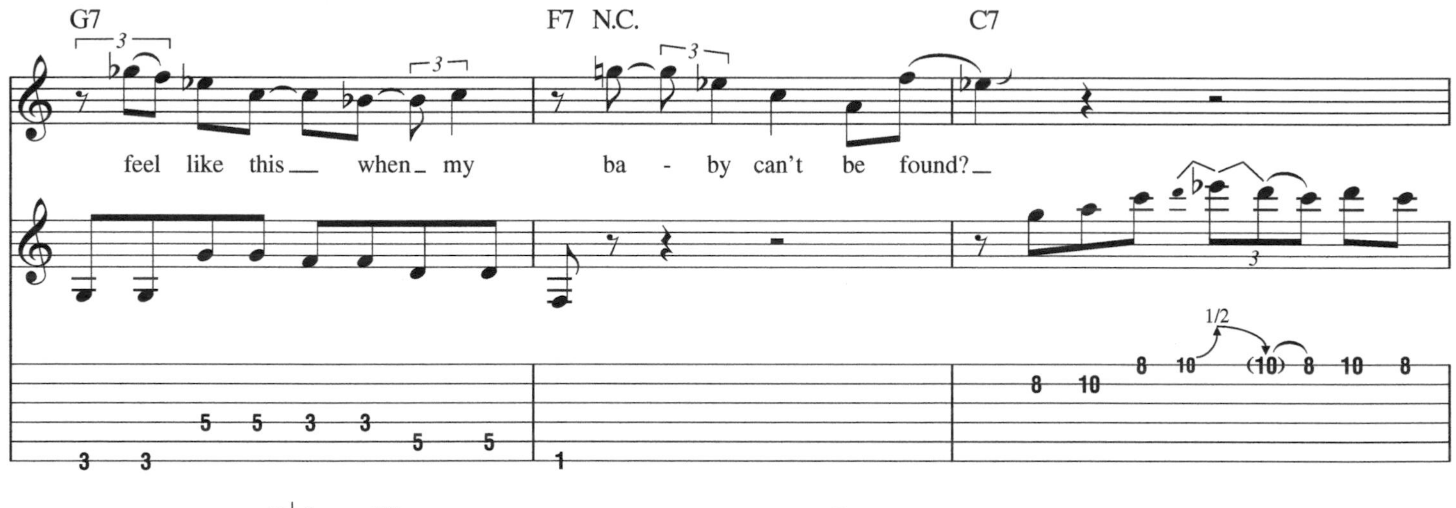

Additional Lyrics

3. Love you, baby, with all my might.
   Love like mine is outta sight.
   I'll lie for you if you want me to.
   I really don't believe that your love is true.

I'm Your Hoochie Coochie Man

Written by Willie Dixon

jump an' shout.
Then the world wan-na know

Chorus
D7
what this all a - bout?"
But you know I'm here.

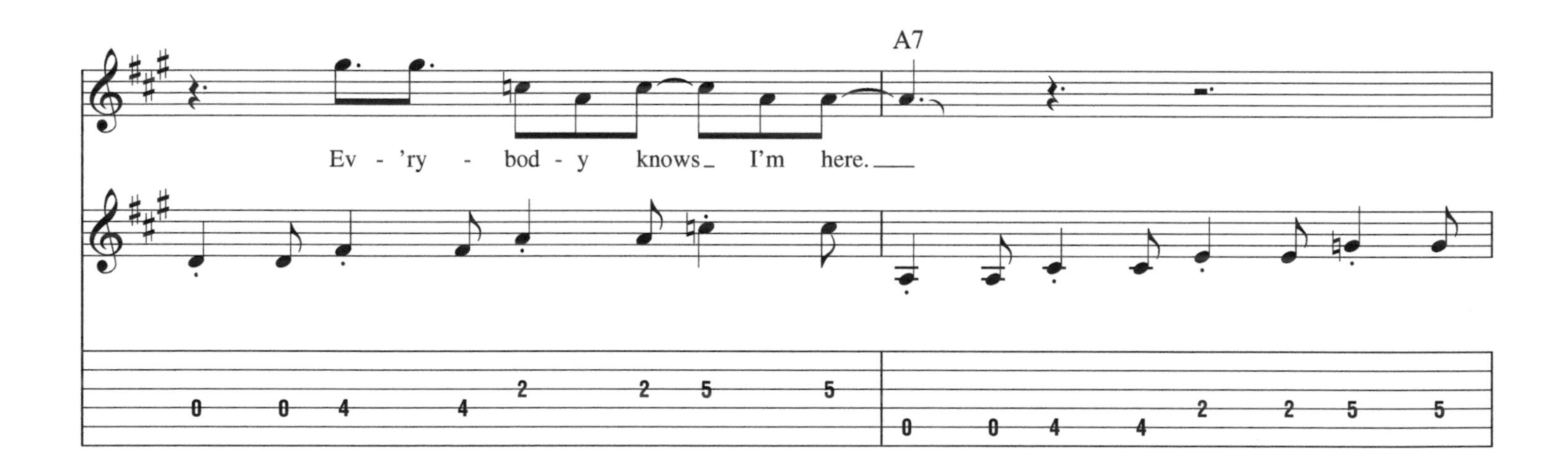
A7
Ev - 'ry - bod - y knows I'm here.

To Coda
E7
Well, you know I'm the Hoo - chie Coo - chie Man,

D7
A7
ev - 'ry - bod - y knows I'm here.

1.
E7
2.
E7
8va

Guitar Solo

A7
8va
D7
hold bend

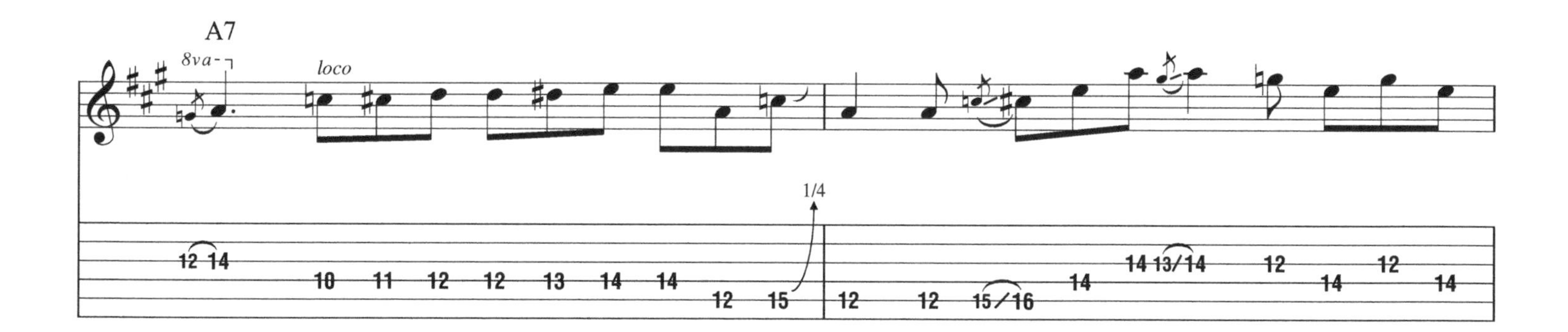
A7
8va
loco
1/4

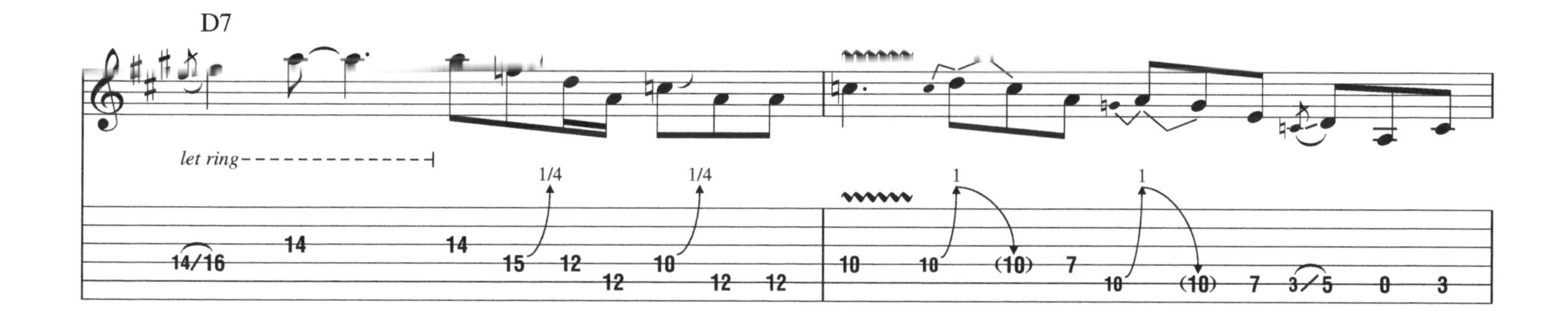
D7
let ring
1/4
1/4
1
1

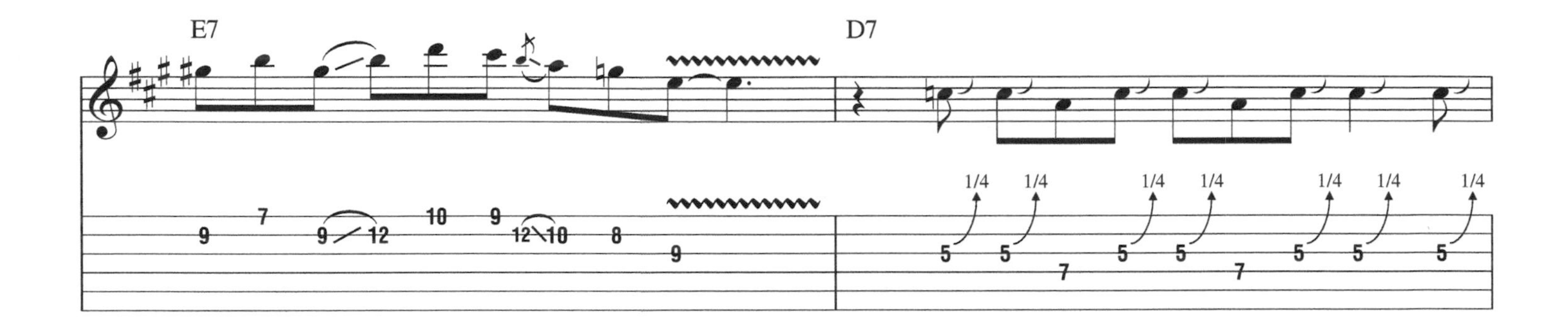

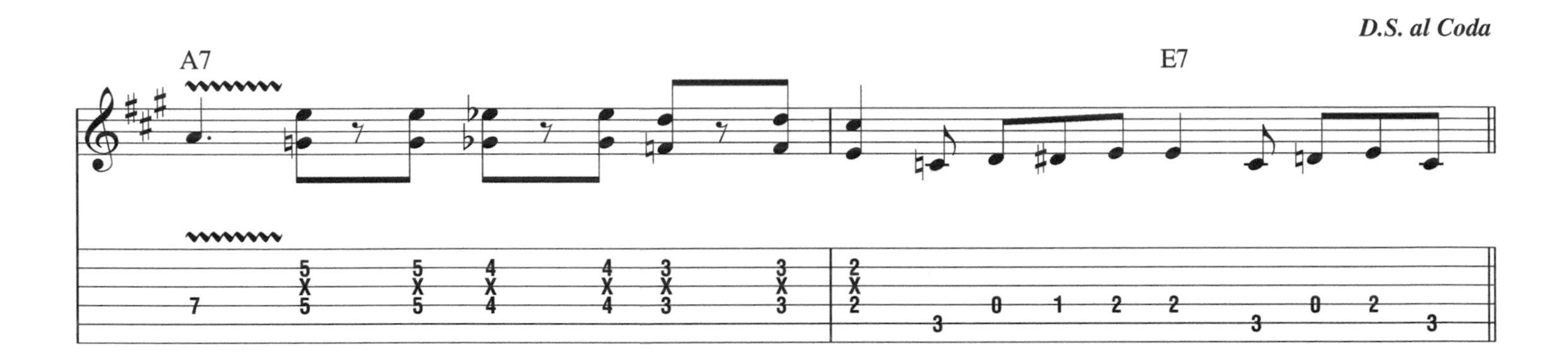

Additional Lyrics

2. I got a black cat bone,
   I got a mojo too.
   I got the John the Conquerroot,
   I'm gonna mess with you.
   I'm gonna make you girls
   Lead me by my hand.
   Then the world'll know
   I'm the Hoochie Coochie man.

3. On the seventh hour,
   On the seventh day,
   On the seventh month,
   The seventh doctor say,
   "You were born for good luck,
   And that you'll see."
   I got seven hundred dollars,
   Don't you mess with me.

Pride and Joy

Written by Stevie Ray Vaughan

Tune down 1/2 step:
(low to high) E♭-A♭-D♭-G♭-B♭-E♭

Intro

Moderate shuffle ♩ = 122

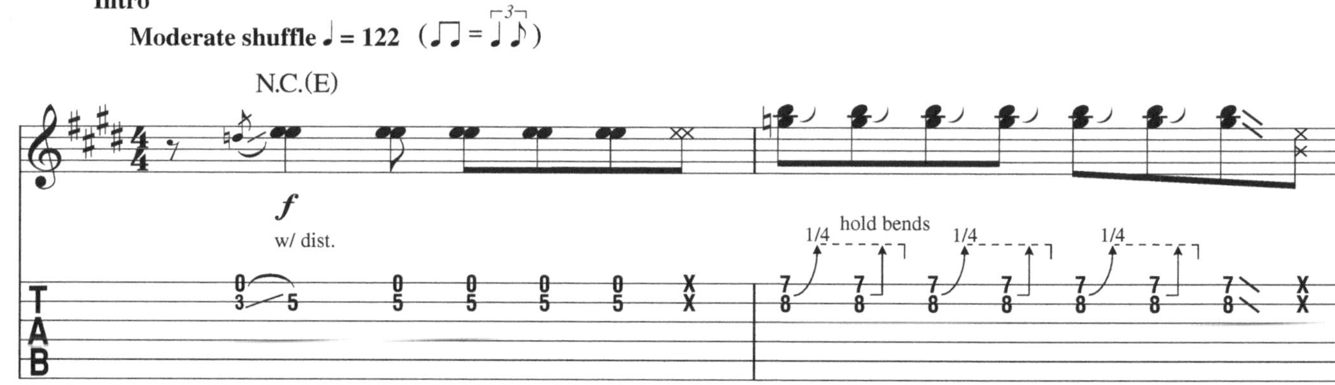

B7

A7
E
B7
1. Well, you've
1/4
* Mute w/ palm of pick hand.

Verse

E
heard a - bout lov - in' giv - in' sight to the blind.
2. See additional lyrics
sim.
1/2
let ring

A7
My ba - by's lov - in' 'cause the sun to shine. An' she's my sweet lit - tle thang,
let ring

E
she('s) my pride and joy.
She('s) my
B7
A7
sweet lit - tle ba - by, I'm her lit - tle lov - er boy.
E
1.
B7
2. Yeah, I
rake
2.
B7
Verse
E N.C.
3. Yeah, I love my la - dy to be
4. See additional lyrics

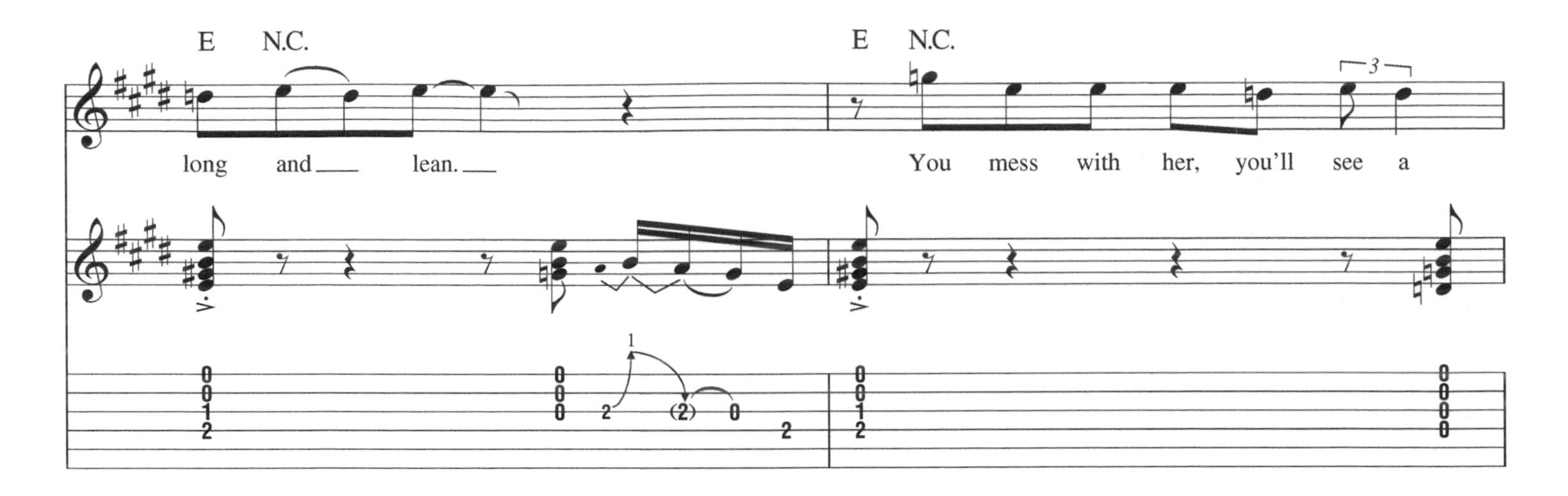
E N.C.
long and lean.
E N.C.
You mess with her, you'll see a

A7
man get - tin' mean.
She('s) my sweet lit - tle thang,

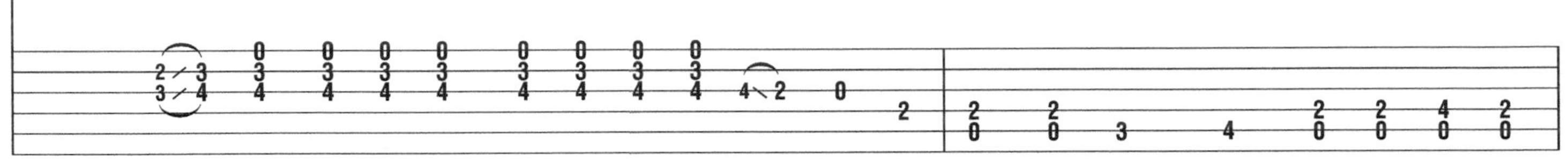

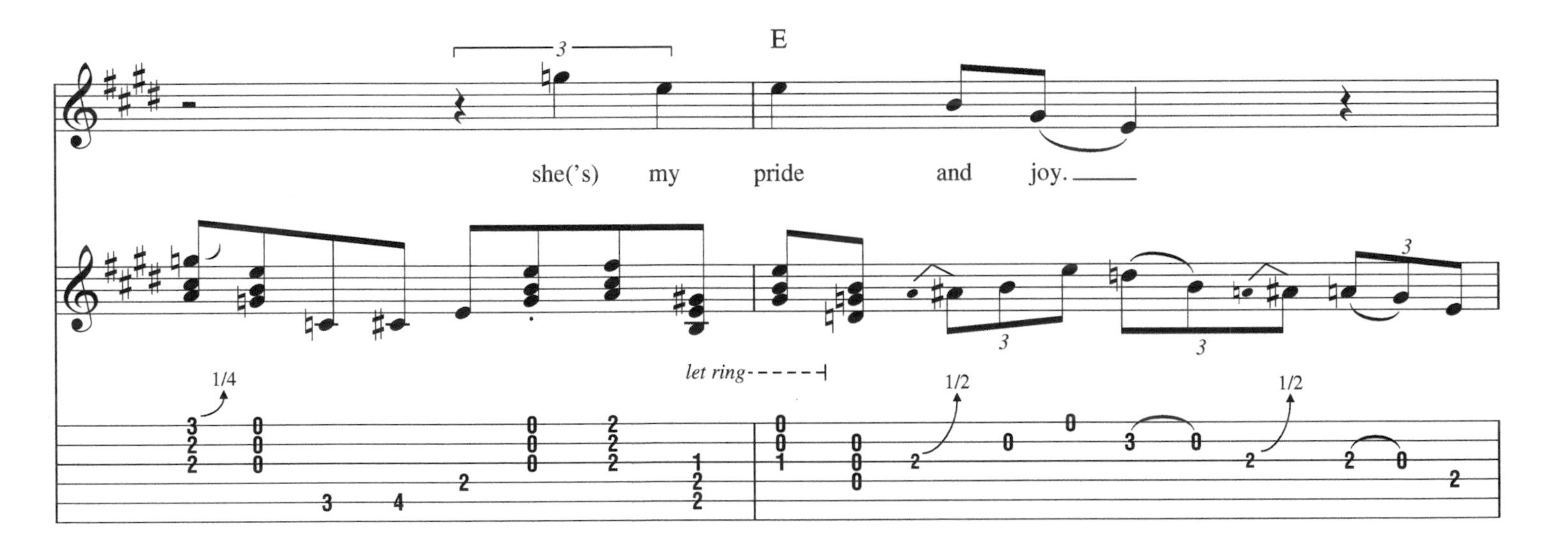
E
she('s) my pride and joy.
let ring

B7
She('s) my sweet lit - tle ba - by, I'm

To Coda 𝄌

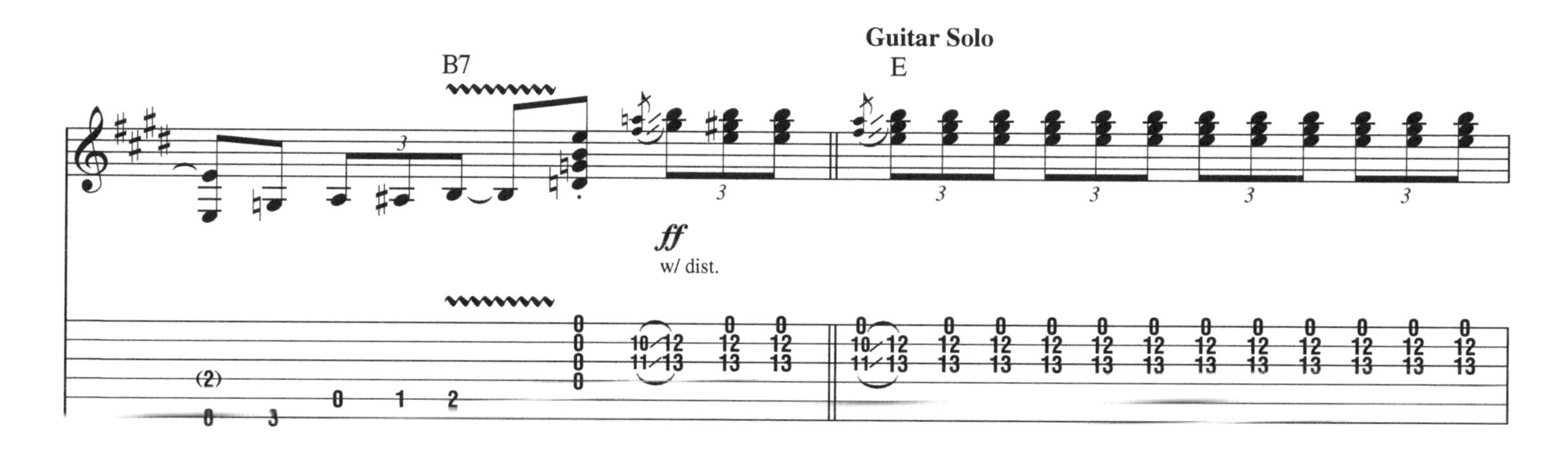

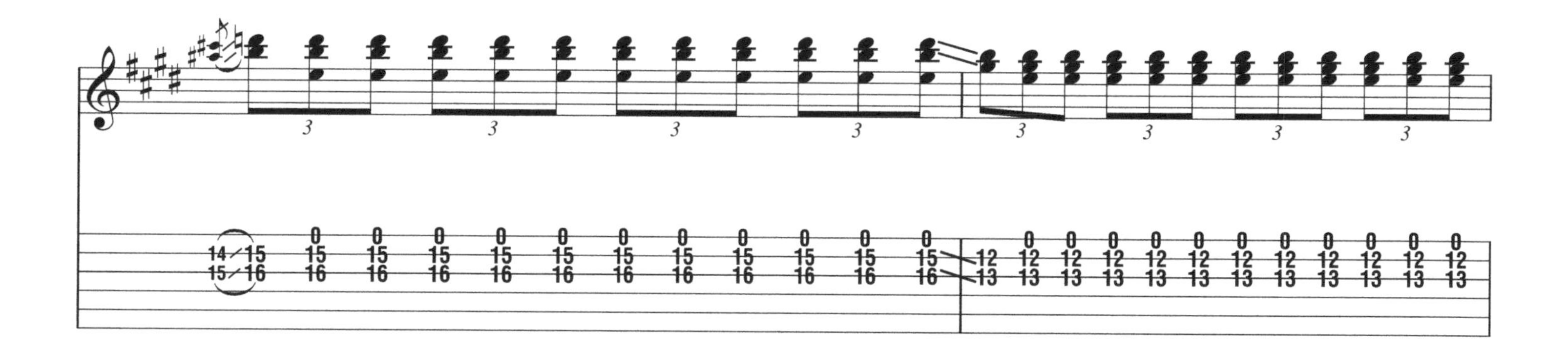

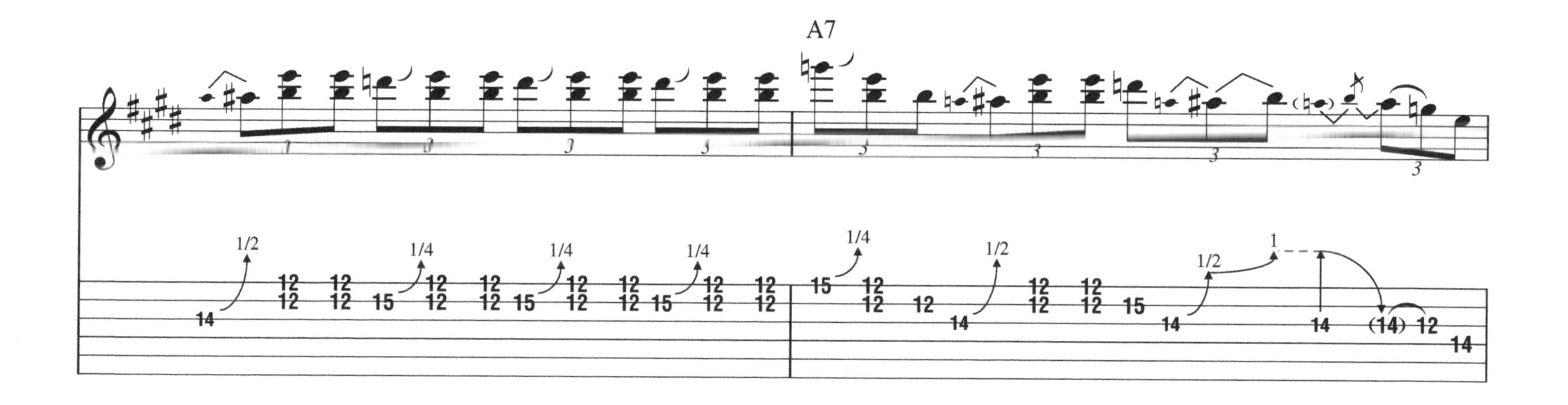

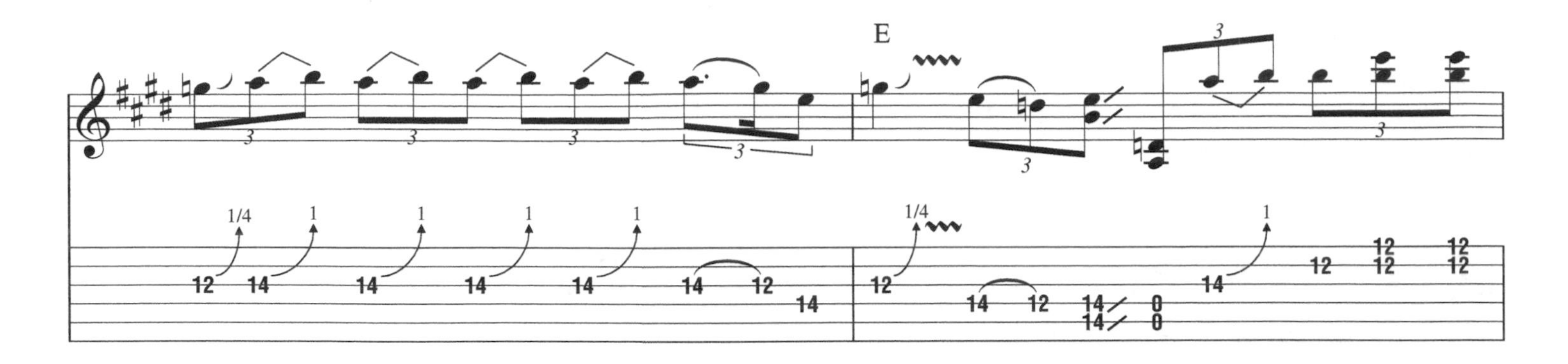
E

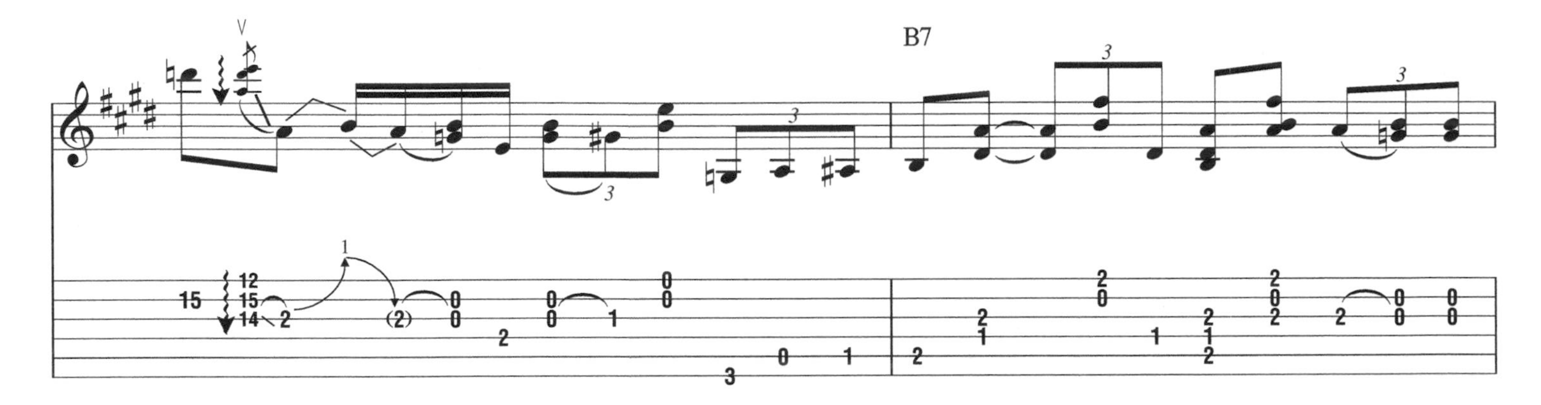
B7

A7
E
rake

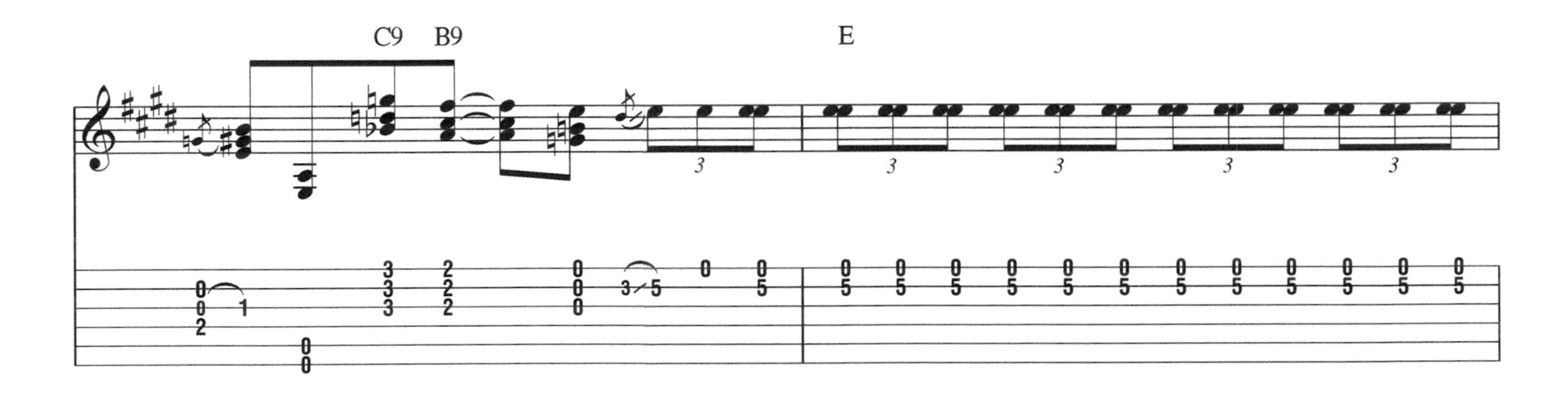
C9
B9
E

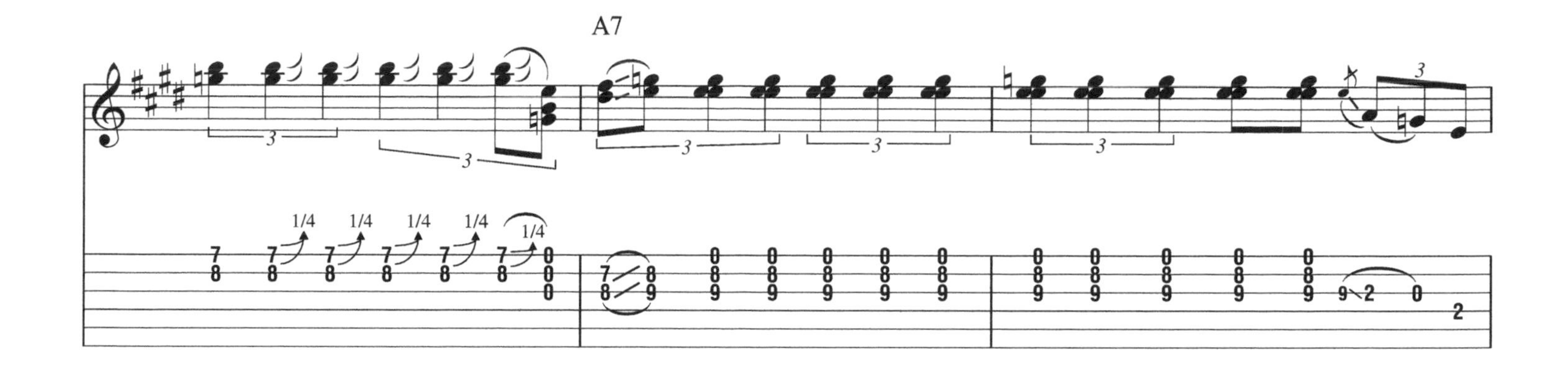
A7

E
let ring
tr

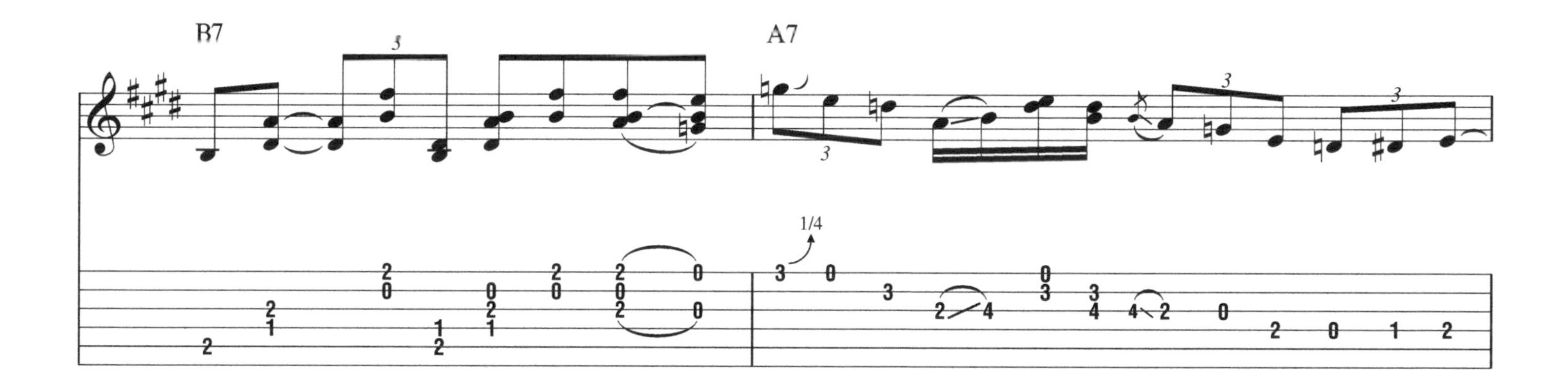
B7
A7

D.S. al Coda
E
B7
4. Well, I
rake
w/ slight dist.

Coda
Verse
B7
E
5. Yeah, I love my ba - by, my heart and soul.

A7
Love like ours ah, won't nev - er grow old. She('s) my sweet lit - tle thang,

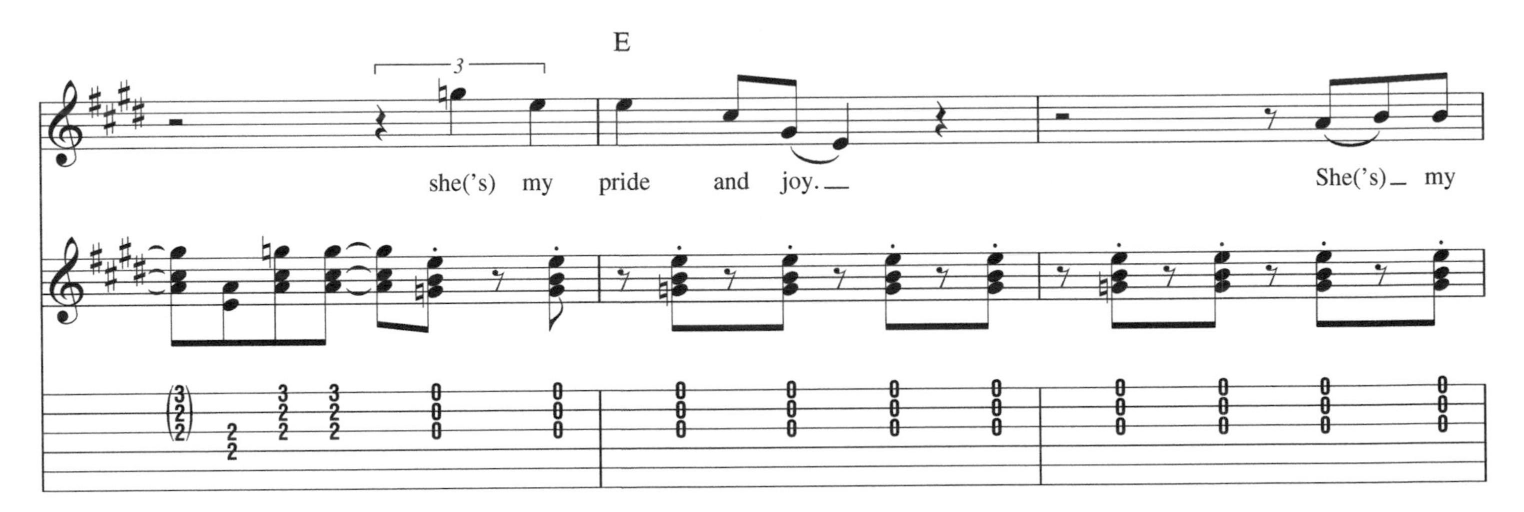
E
she('s) my pride and joy. She('s) my

B7
A7
E
sweet lit-tle ba - by, I'm her lit - tle lov - er boy.
rake

Guitar Solo
B7
E7
ff
w/ dist.

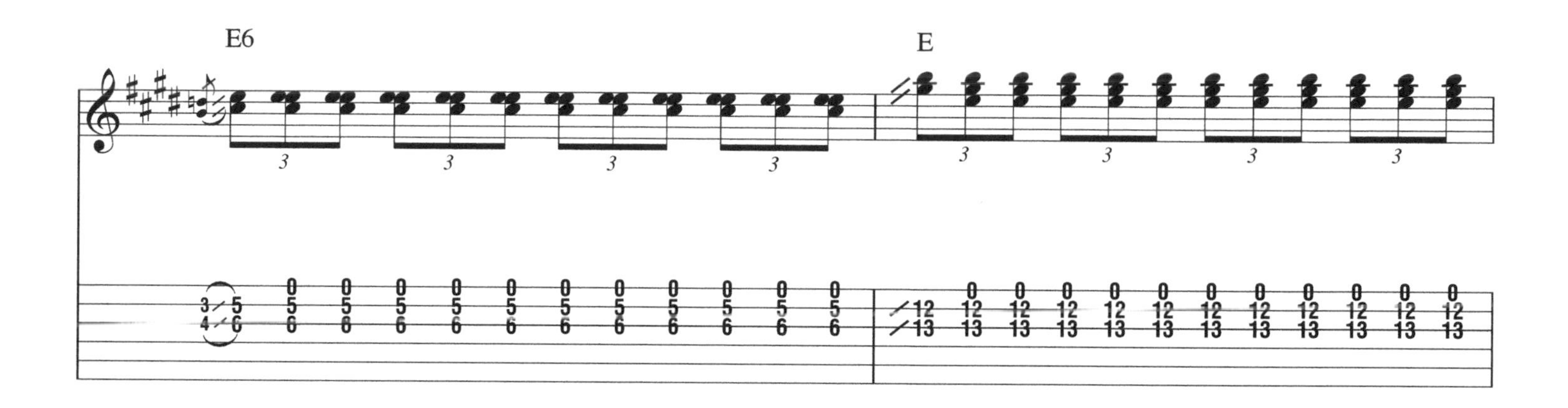
E6
E

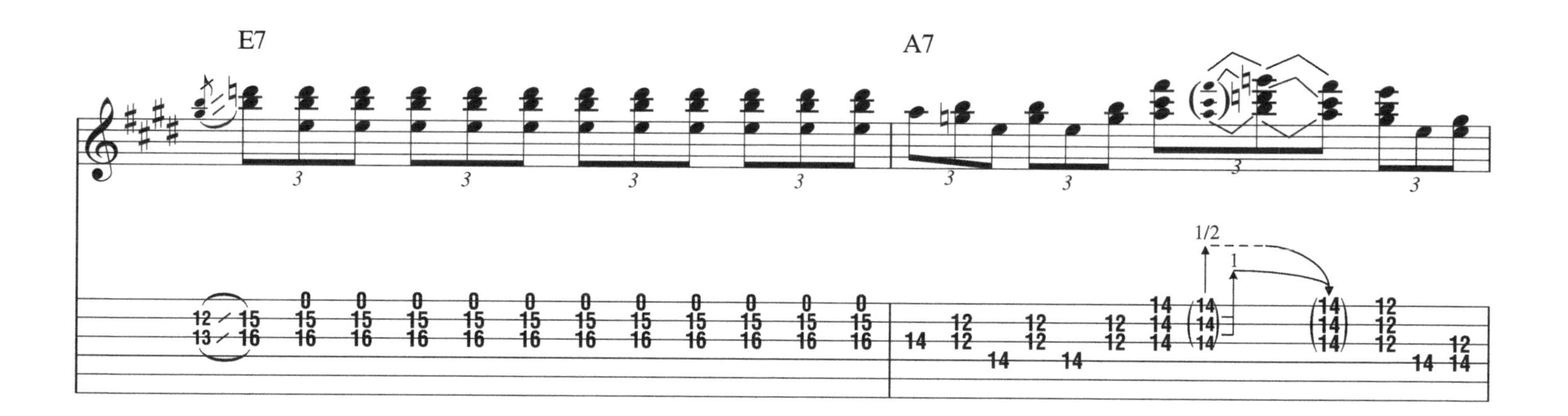
E7
A7

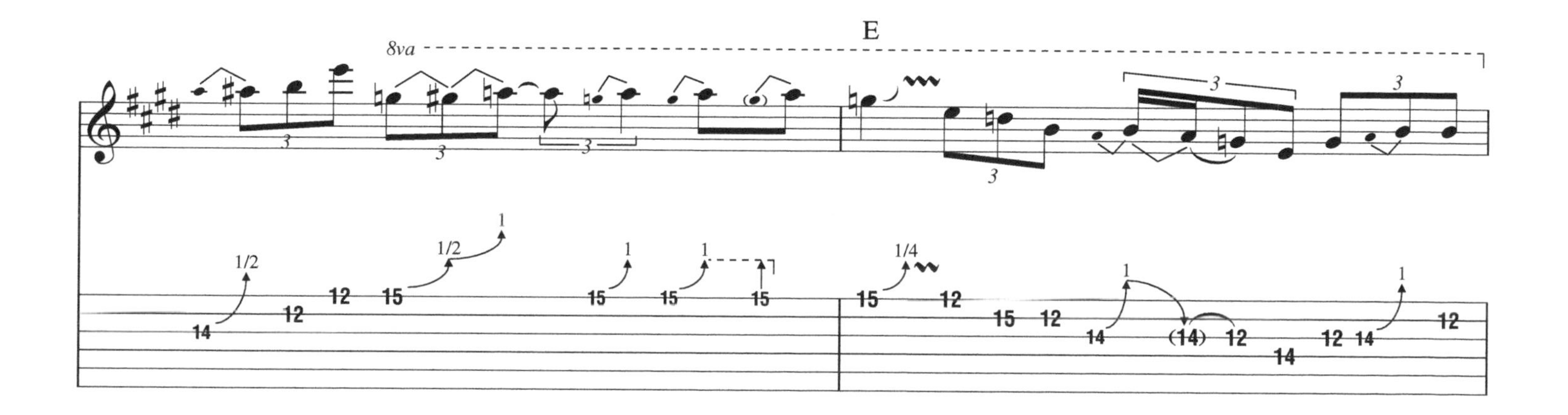
8va
E

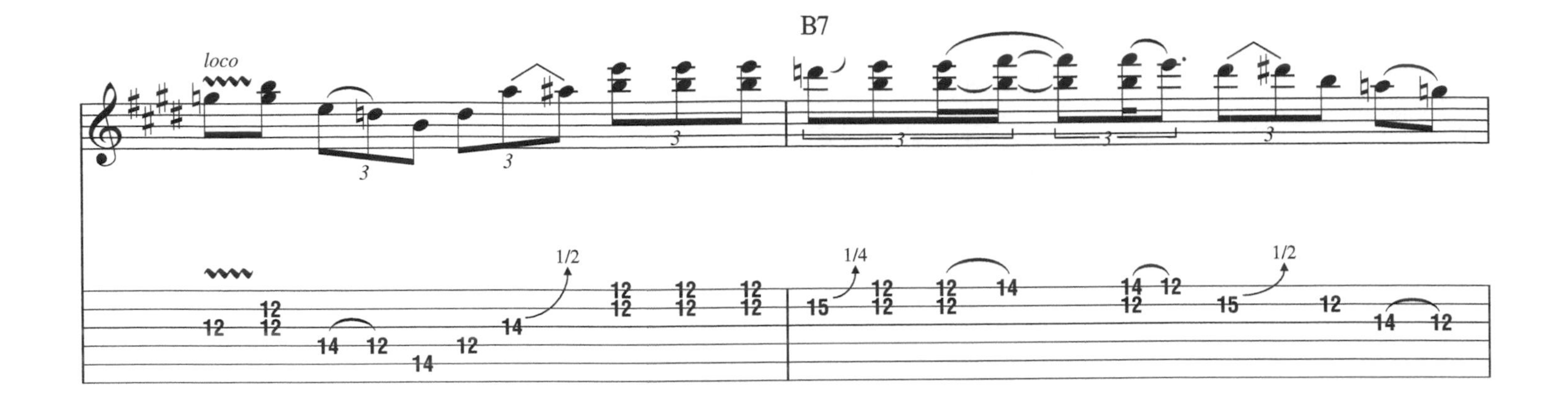

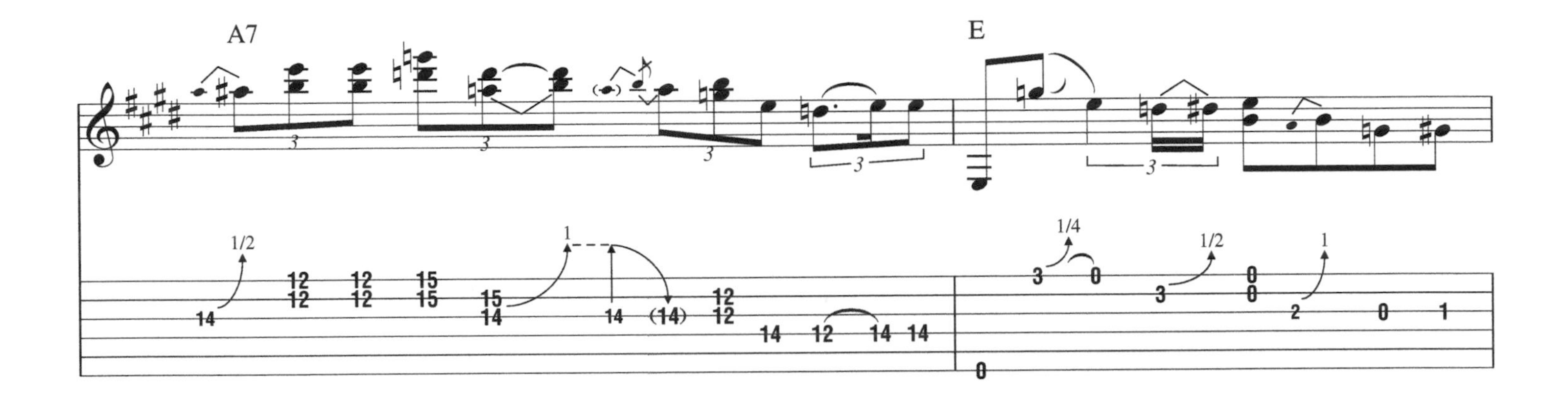

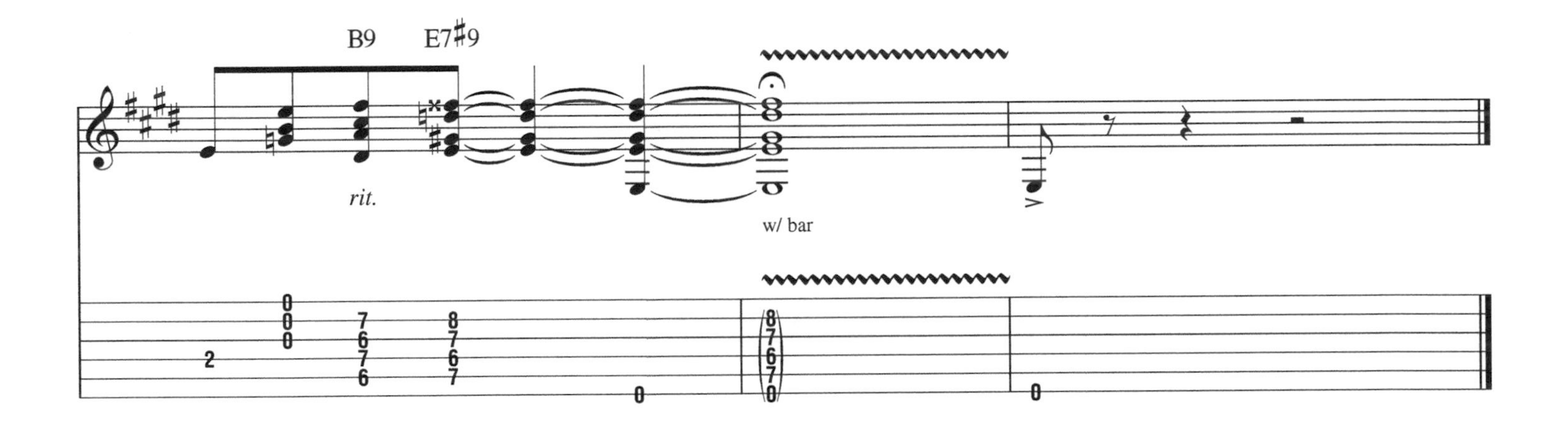

Additional Lyrics

2. Yeah, I love my baby, my heart and soul.
   Love like ours ah, won't never grow old.
   She('s) me sweet little thang,
   She('s) my pride and joy.
   She('s) my sweet little baby,
   I'm her little lover boy.

4. Well, I love my baby like the finest w, wine.
   Stick with her until the end of time.
   An' she's my sweet little thang,
   She('s) my pride and joy.
   She('s) my sweet little baby,
   I'm her little lover boy.

Sweet Home Chicago

Words and Music by Robert Johnson

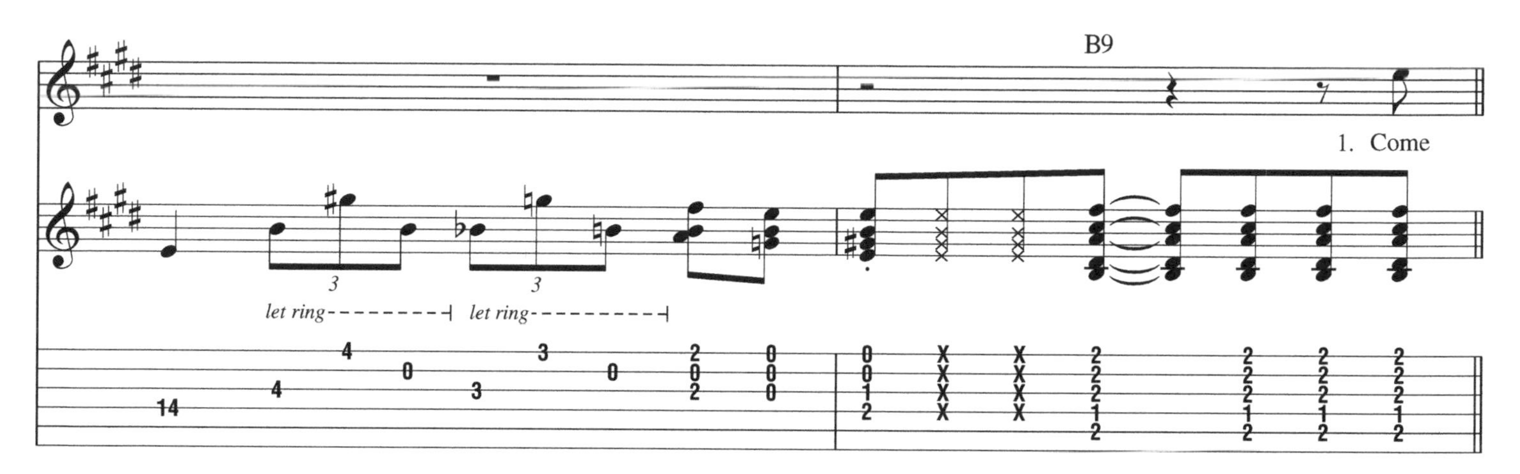

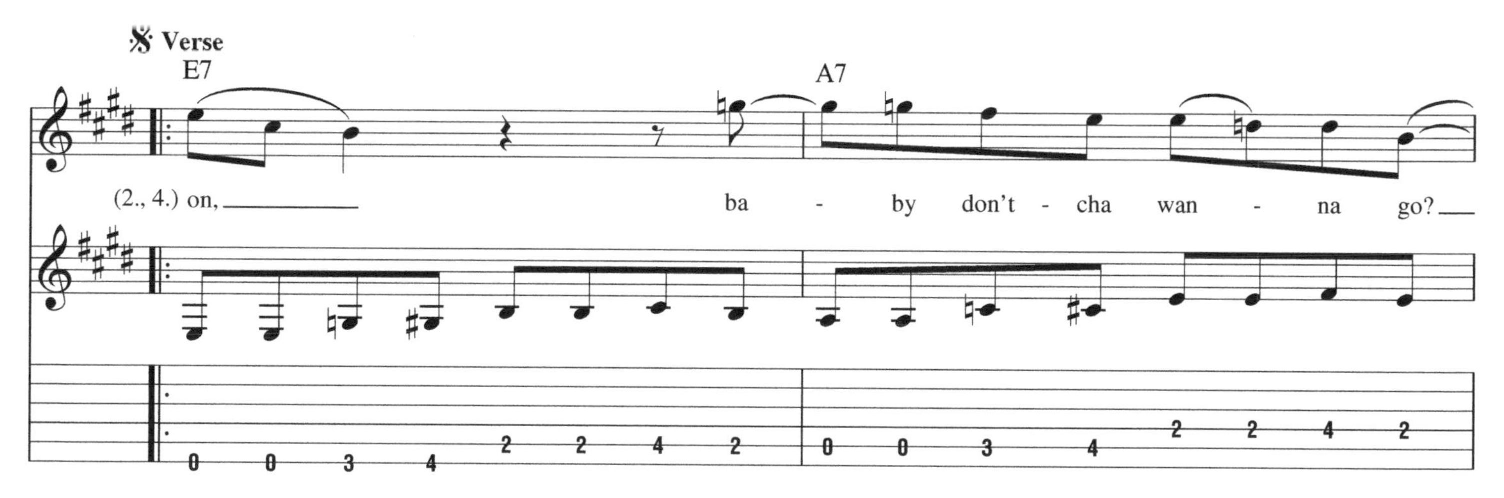

A7
ba - by don't - cha wan - na go
0 0 3 4 2 2 4 2
0 0 3 4 2 2 4 2

E7
back to that
3
0 0 3 4 2 2 4 2
0 0 3 4 2 2 4 2

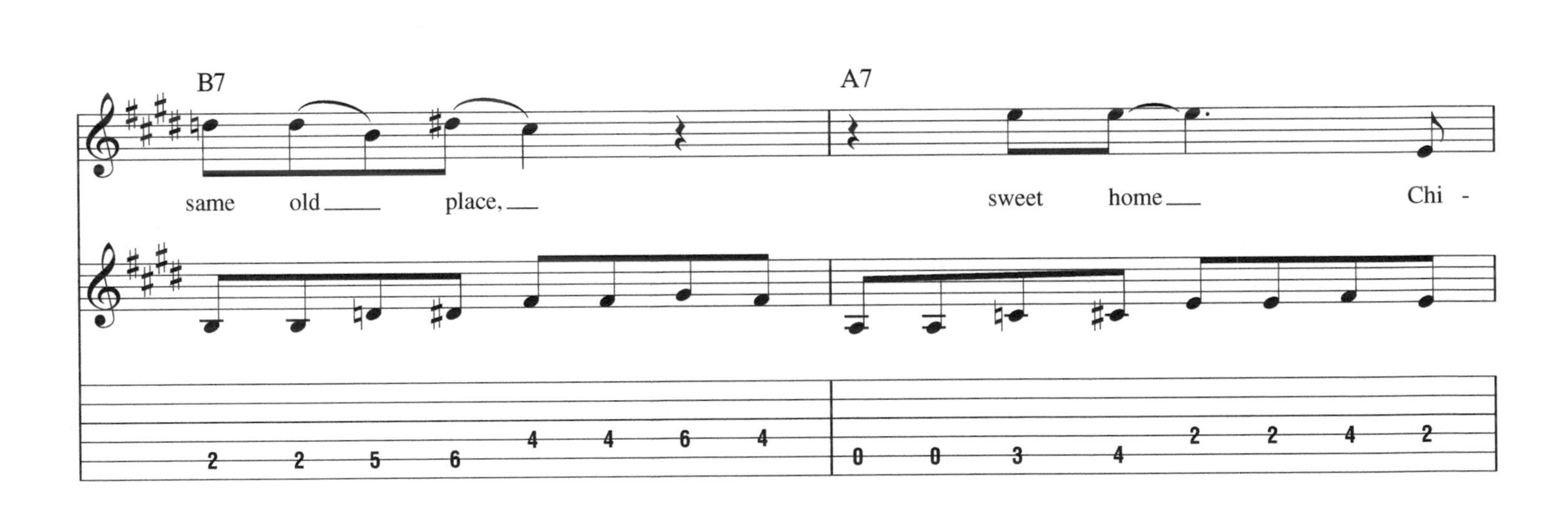
B7
A7
same old place,
sweet home Chi -
2 2 5 6 4 4 6 4
0 0 3 4 2 2 4 2

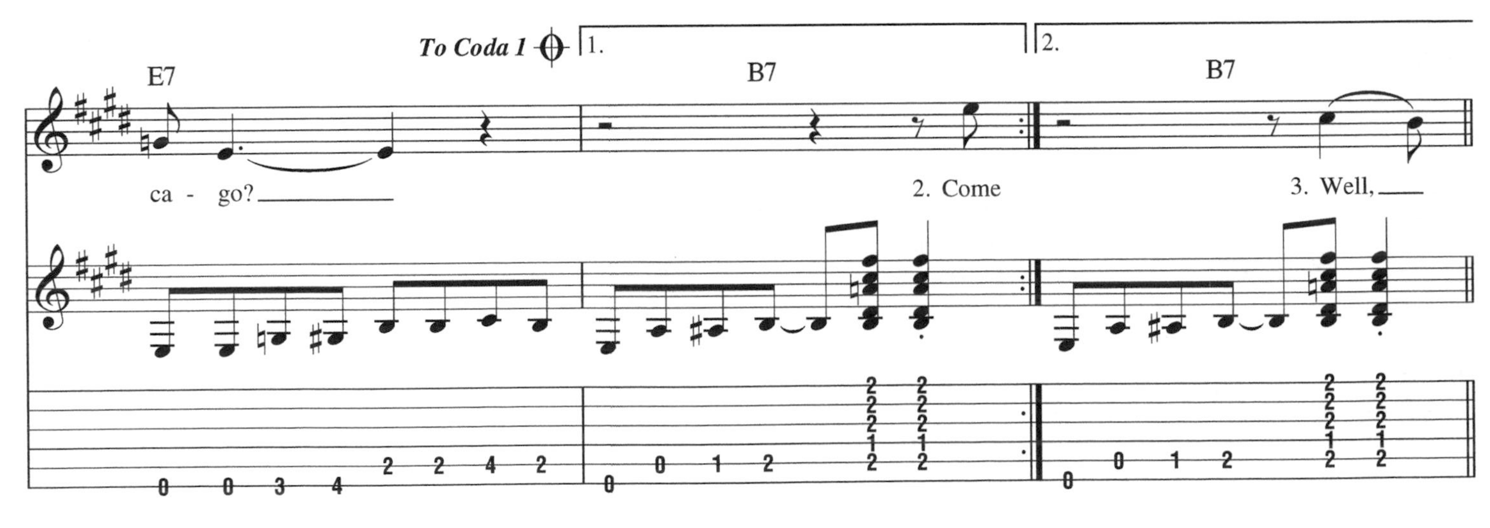
To Coda 1
1.
2.
E7
B7
B7
ca - go?
2. Come
3. Well,

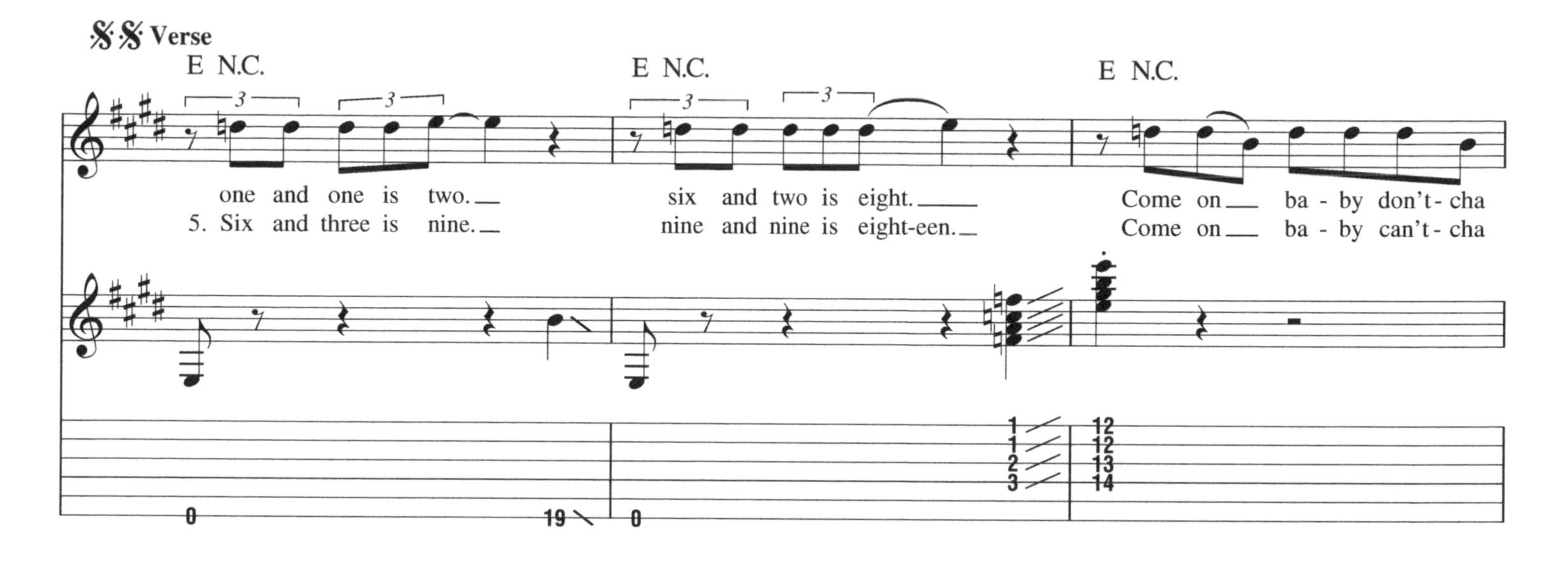
Verse
E N.C.
one and one is two.
5. Six and three is nine.
E N.C.
six and two is eight.
nine and nine is eight-een.
E N.C.
Come on ba - by don't - cha
Come on ba - by can't - cha

E
make me late!
see what I mean!
A7
Hey, ba - by don't - cha wan - na go

E7
B7
back to that same old place,

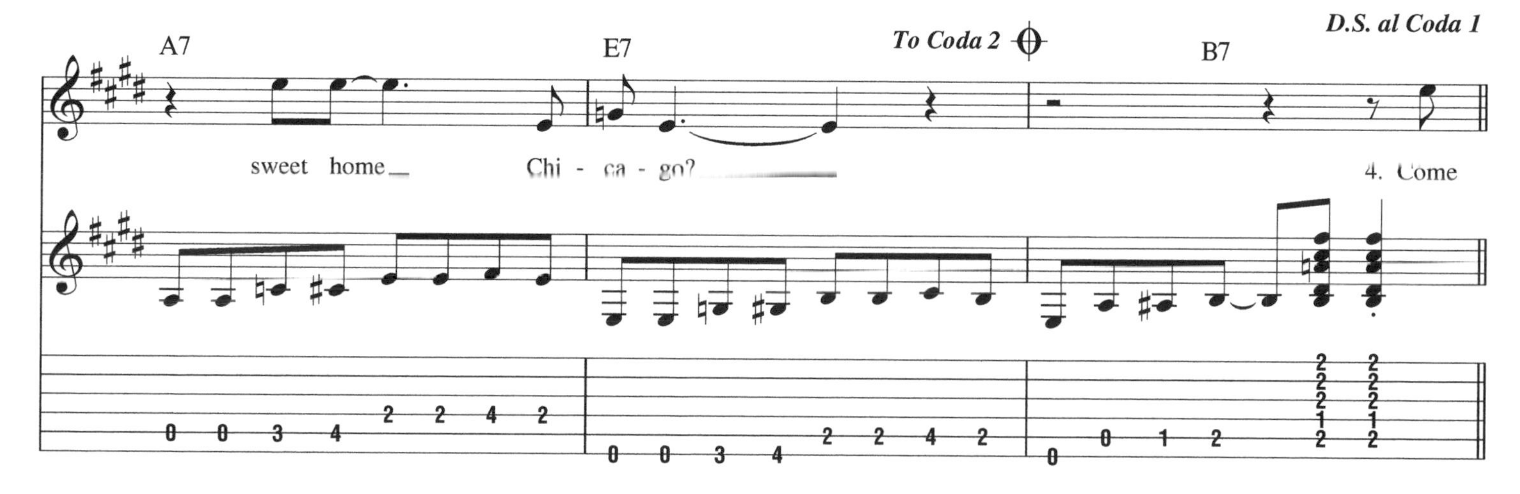
A7
E7
To Coda 2
D.S. al Coda 1
B7
sweet home Chi - ca - go?
4. Come

Coda 1

*Hammer from nowhere. (Don't pick.)

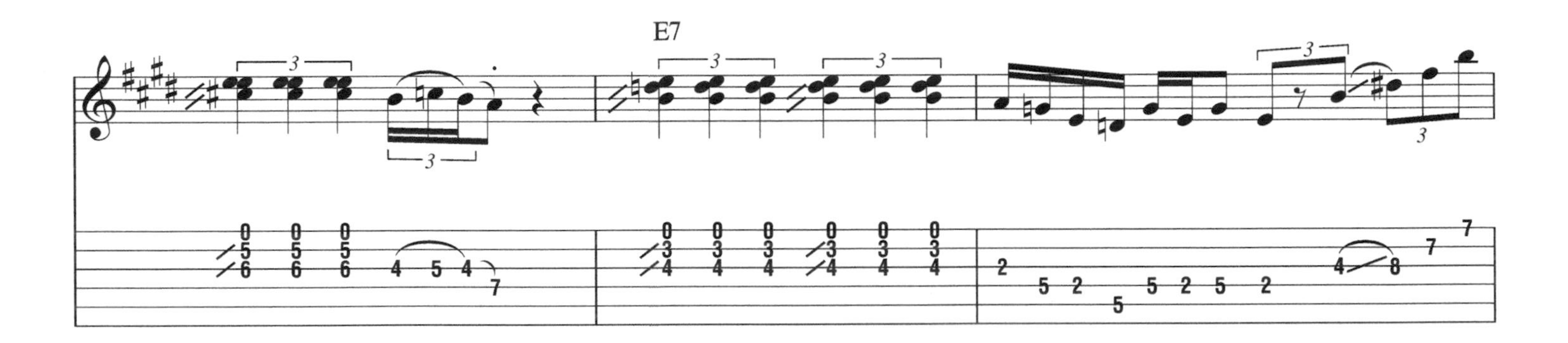

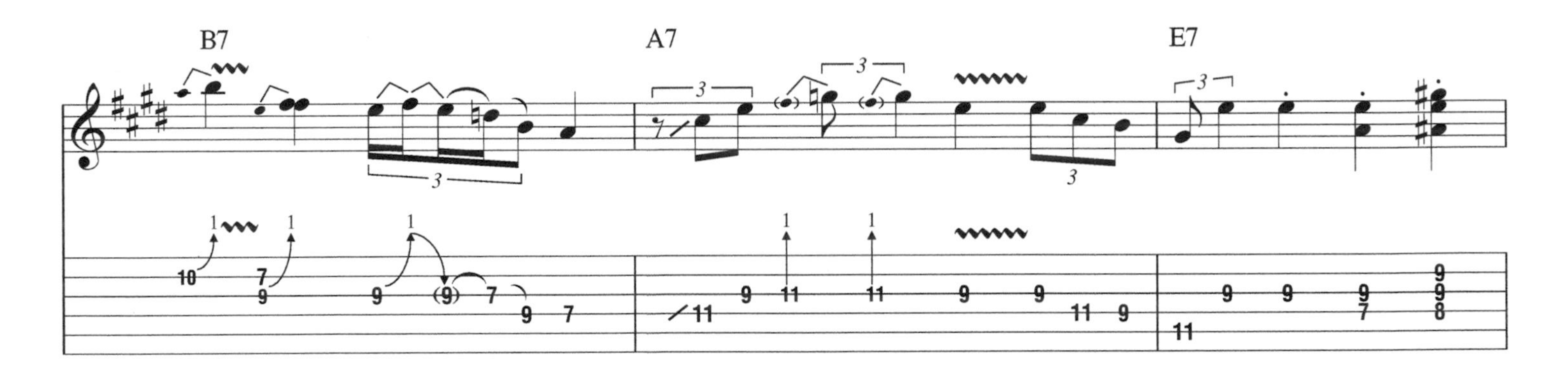

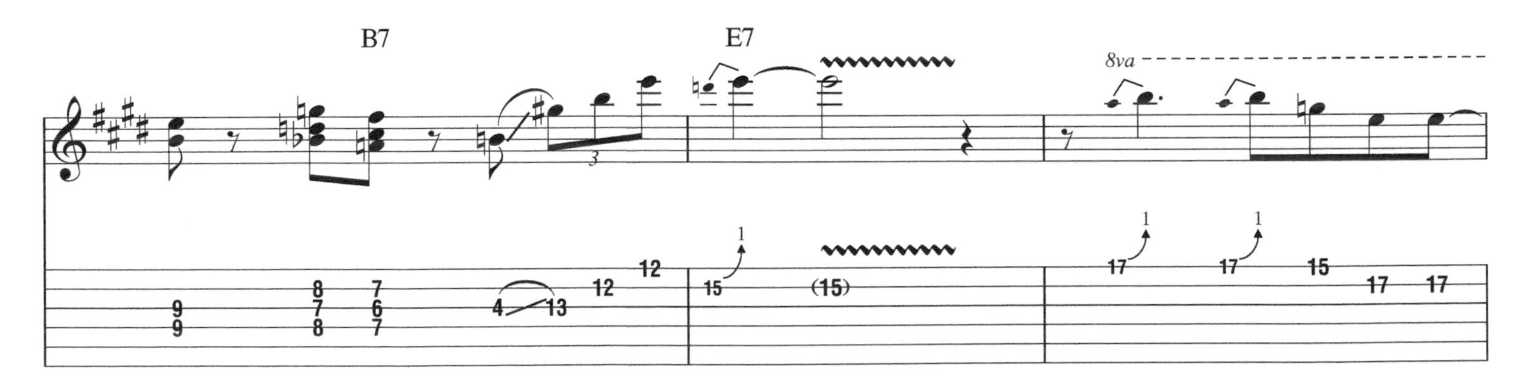

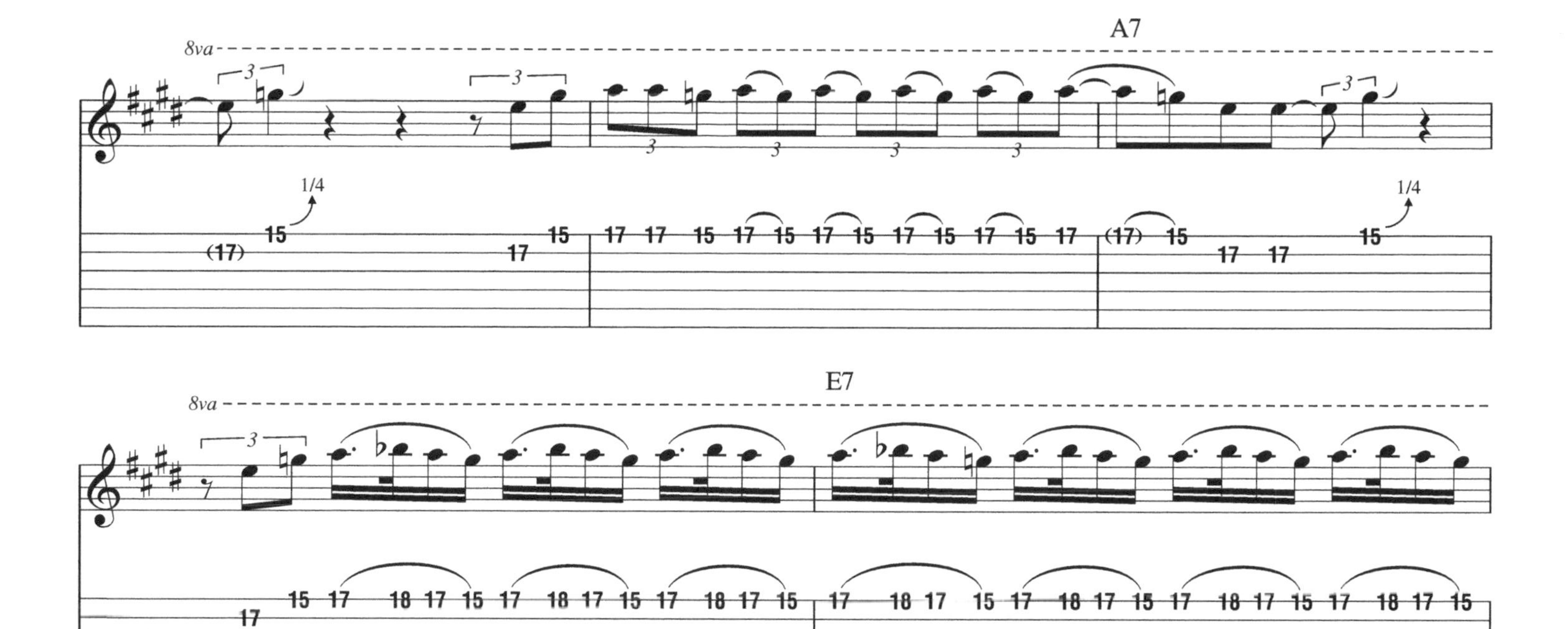
8va
A7
E7

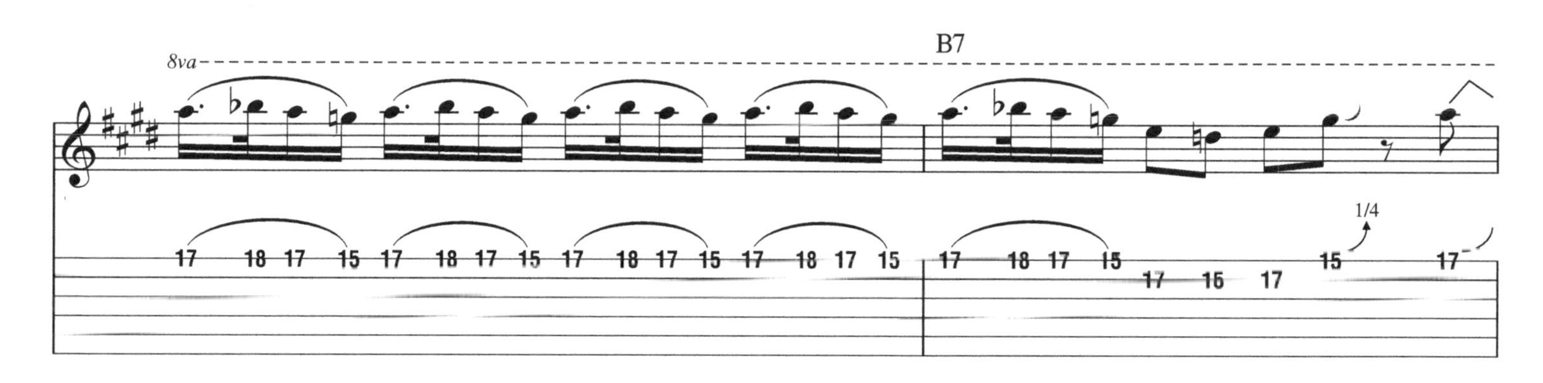
8va
B7

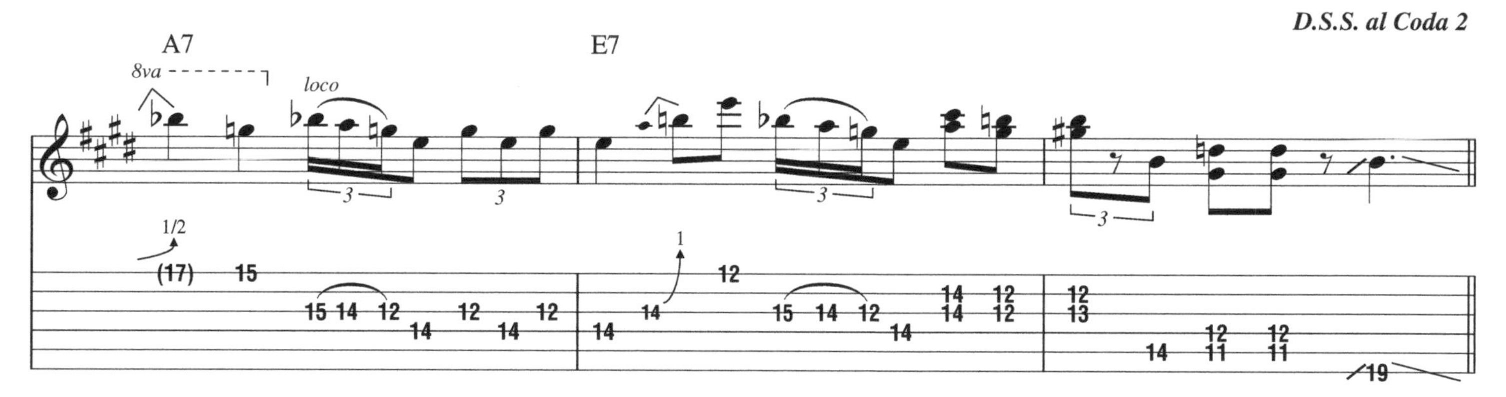
A7
E7
8va
loco
D.S.S. al Coda 2

Coda 2

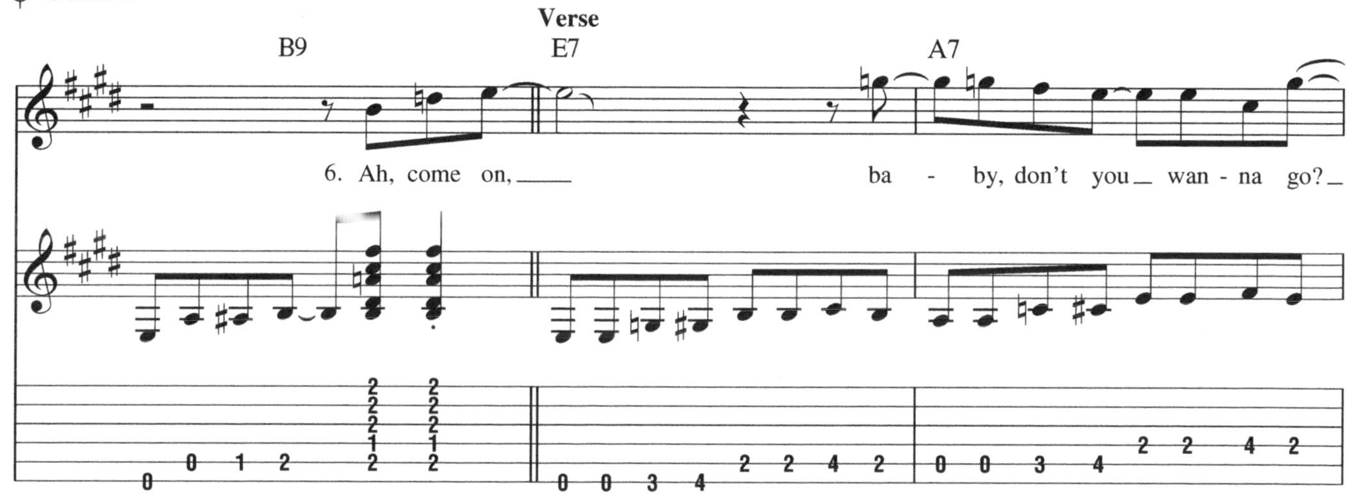
Verse
B9
E7
A7
6. Ah, come on, baby, don't you wan-na go?

E7
A7
Come on,
ba -

E7
- by, don't you wan - na go
back to that

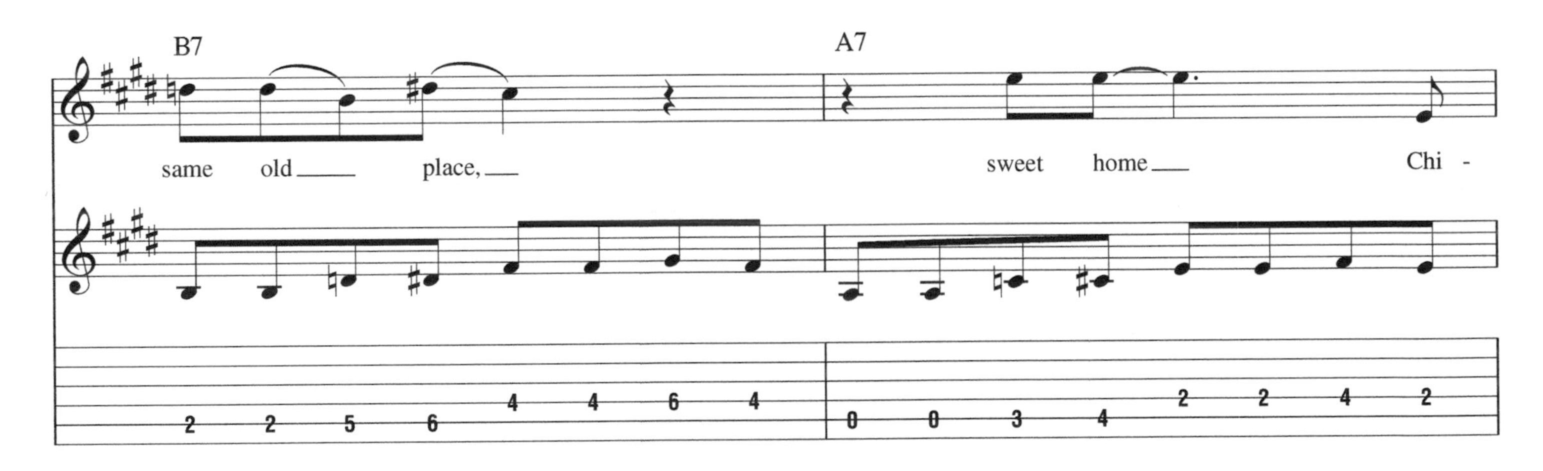
B7
A7
same old place,
sweet home
Chi -

E7
F9
E9
ca - go?

The Thrill Is Gone

Words and Music by Roy Hawkins and Rick Darnell

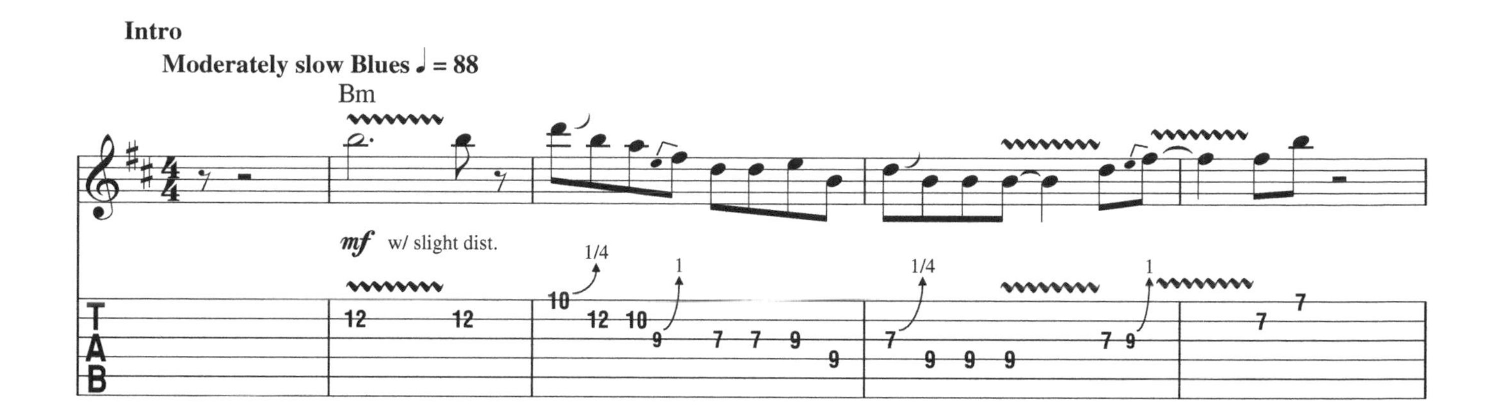

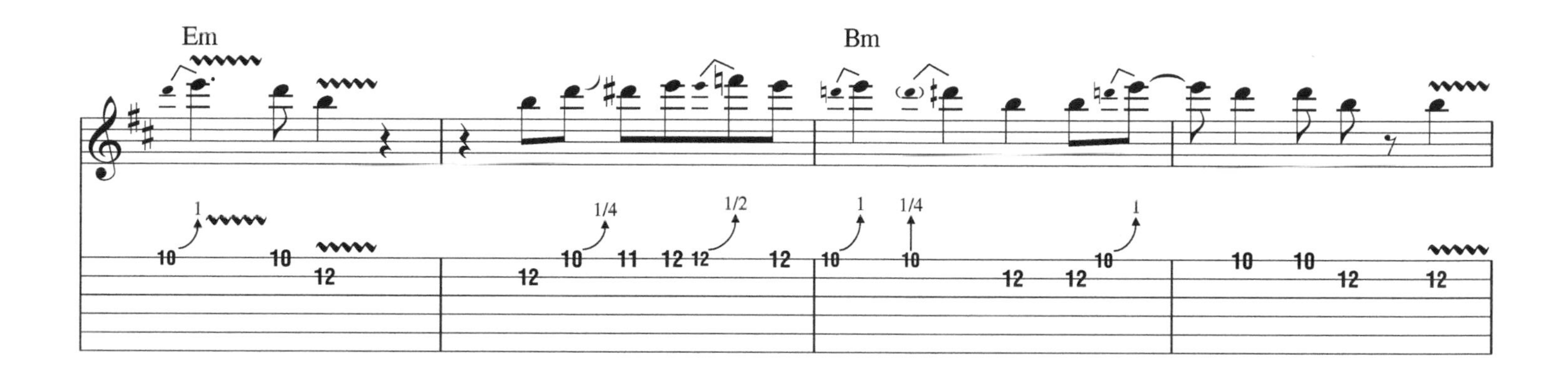

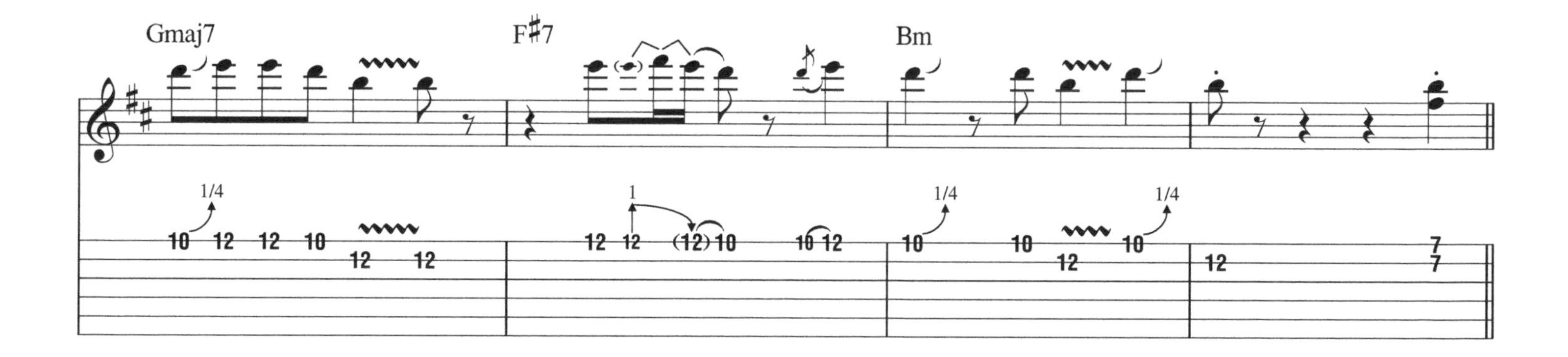

Em
The thrill is gone, baby, the thrill is gone
Bm
away.
Gmaj7
You know you done me wrong, ba-
F#7
by,
Bm
and you'll be sor-ry some day.
To Coda
mp
9 7

Verse
Bm
2. The thrill is gone,
it's gone a-way from me.
7
7
7 10 10 10 10
1

Em
The thrill is gone, baby,
the thrill has
3
1 1 1 1
10 10 10 10
1 1/4
10 10 12

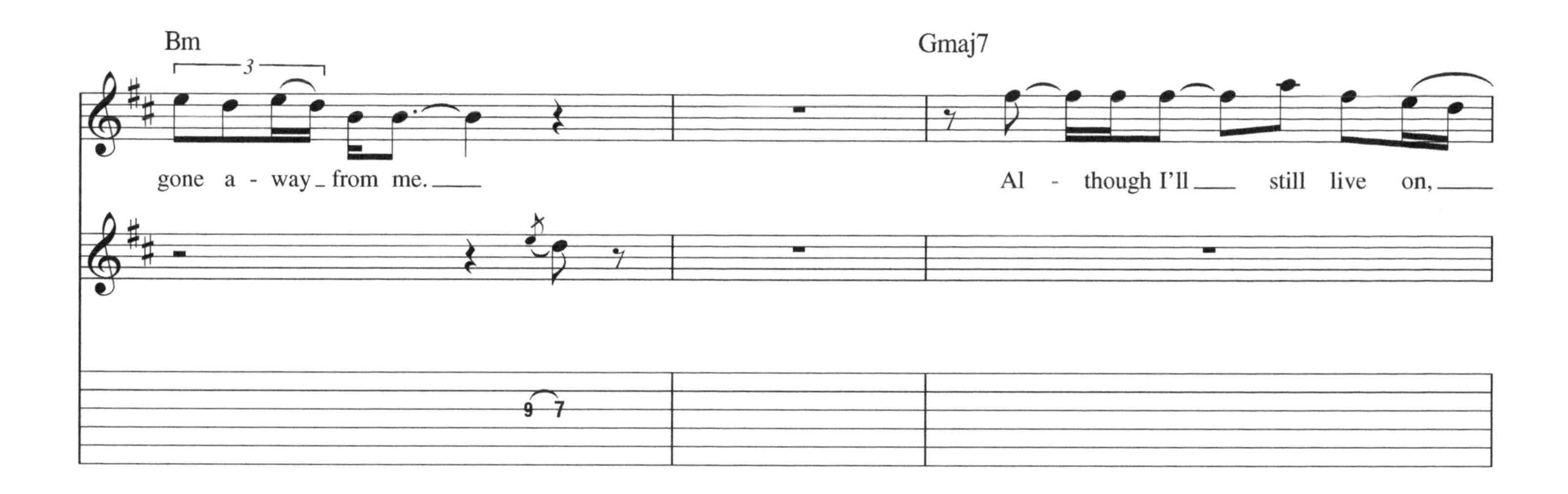
Bm
Gmaj7
gone a - way from me.
Al - though I'll still live on,

F#7
Bm
but so lone - ly I'll be.
mf

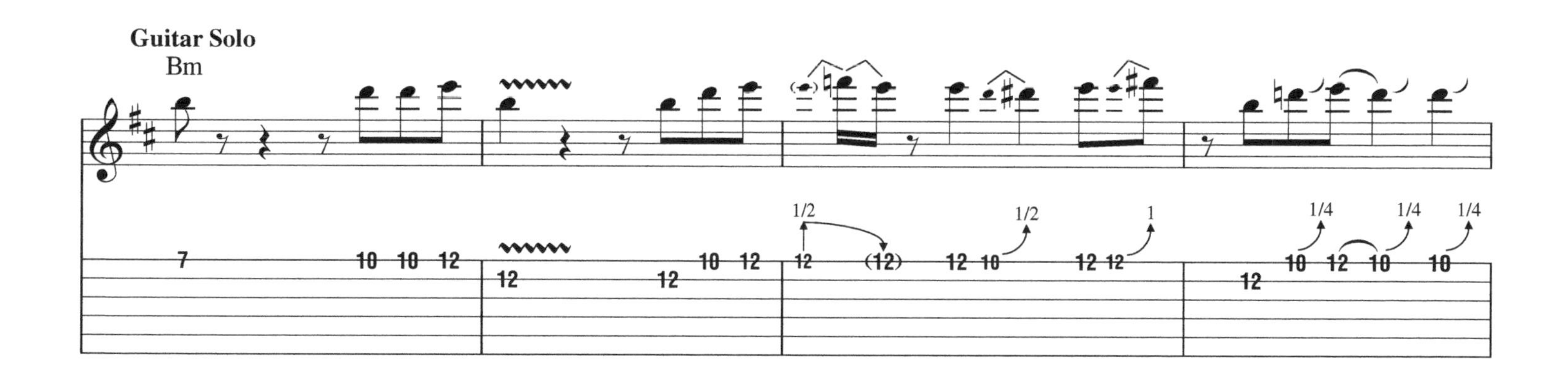
Guitar Solo
Bm

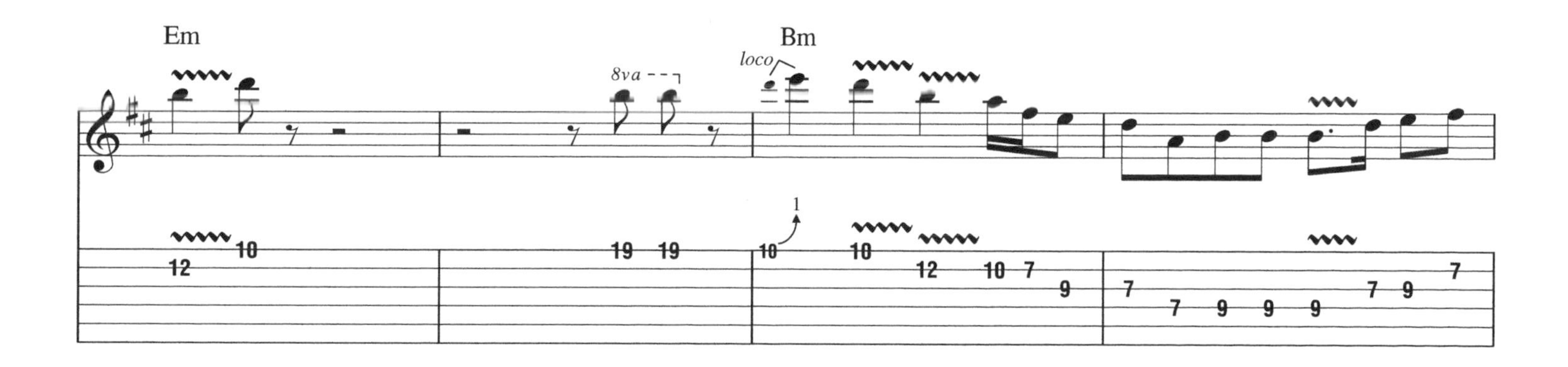
Em
8va
loco
Bm

D.S. al Coda

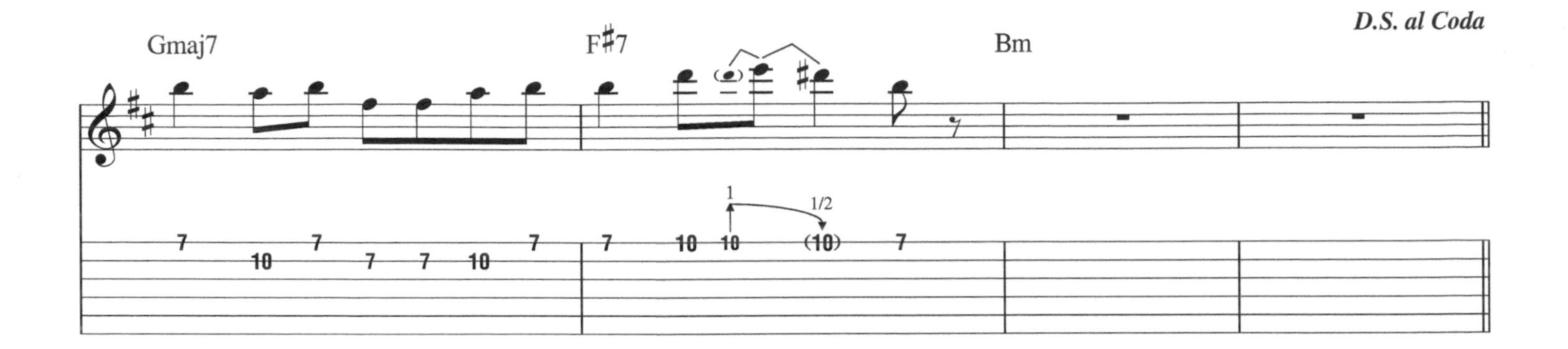
Gmaj7
F♯7
Bm

Coda
Verse
Bm
should.
4. You know I'm free, free now, ba - by.

Em
I'm free from your spell.
Whoa, I'm free, free, free now, I'm free

Bm
Gmaj7
from your spell.
And now that it's all o - ver

F♯7
Bm
all I can do
is wish you
well.
7
7

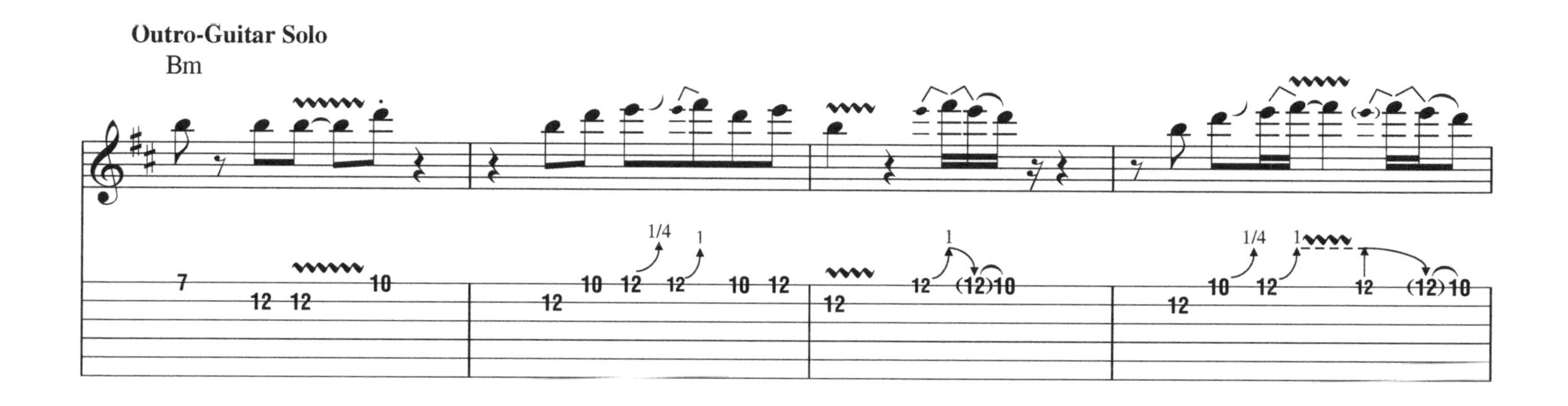
Outro-Guitar Solo
Bm

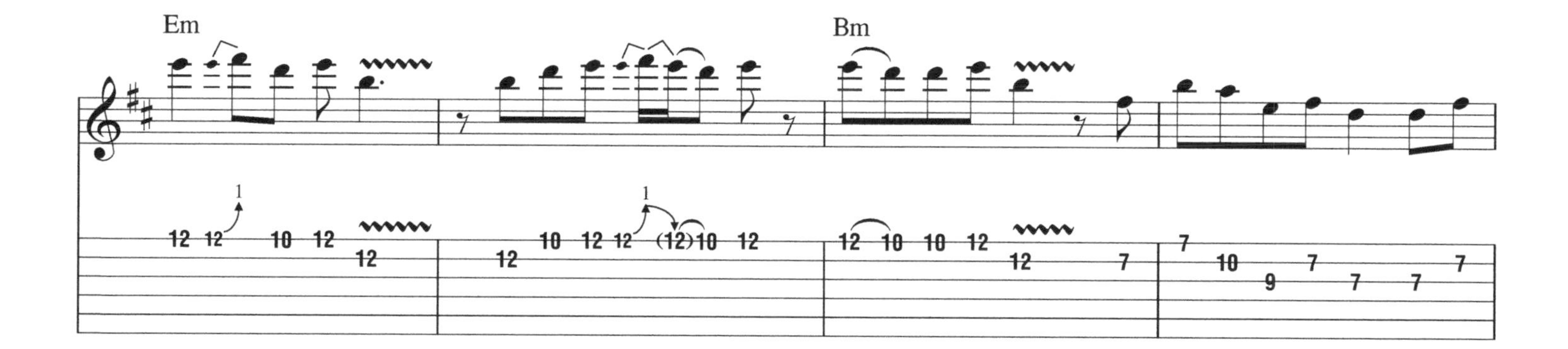
Em
Bm

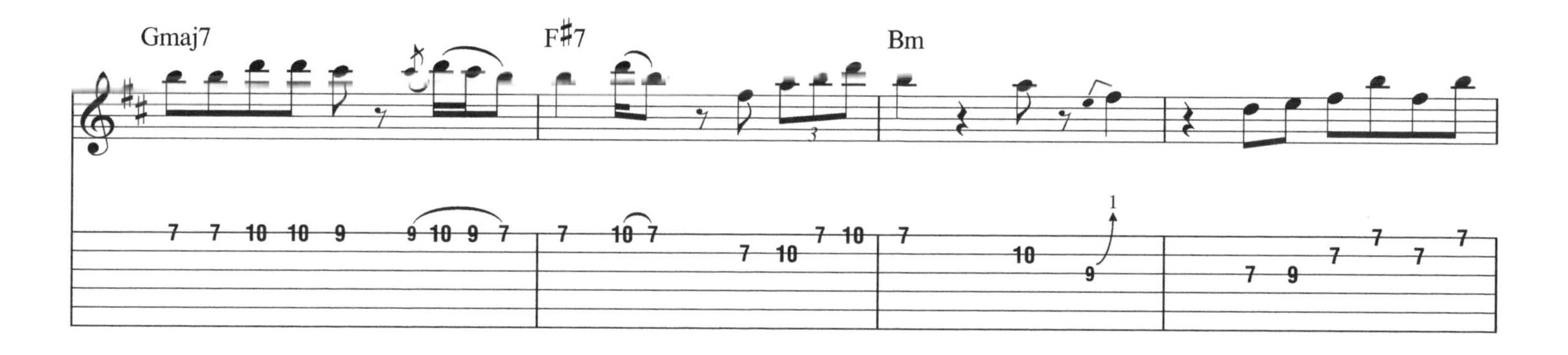
Gmaj7
F♯7
Bm

8va

8va
loco

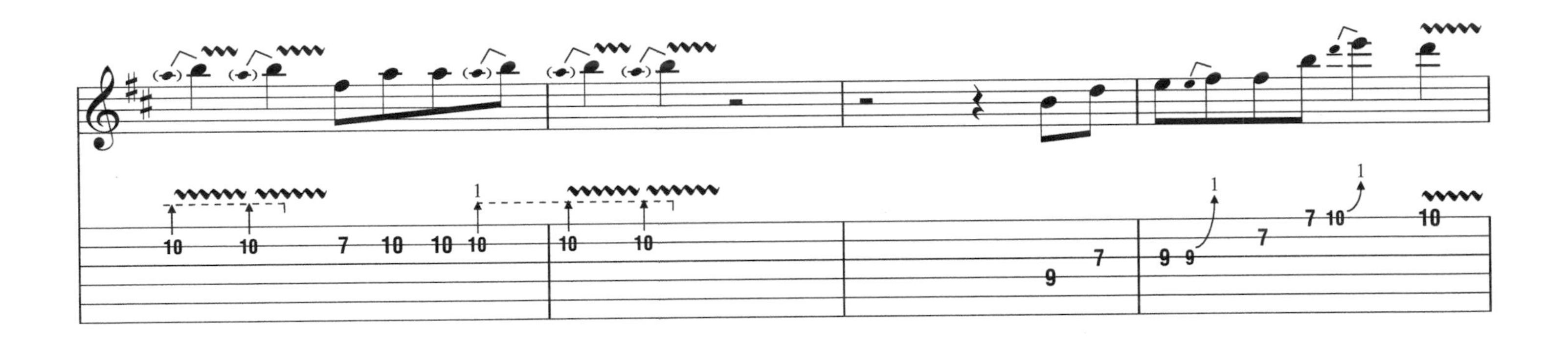

Begin fade

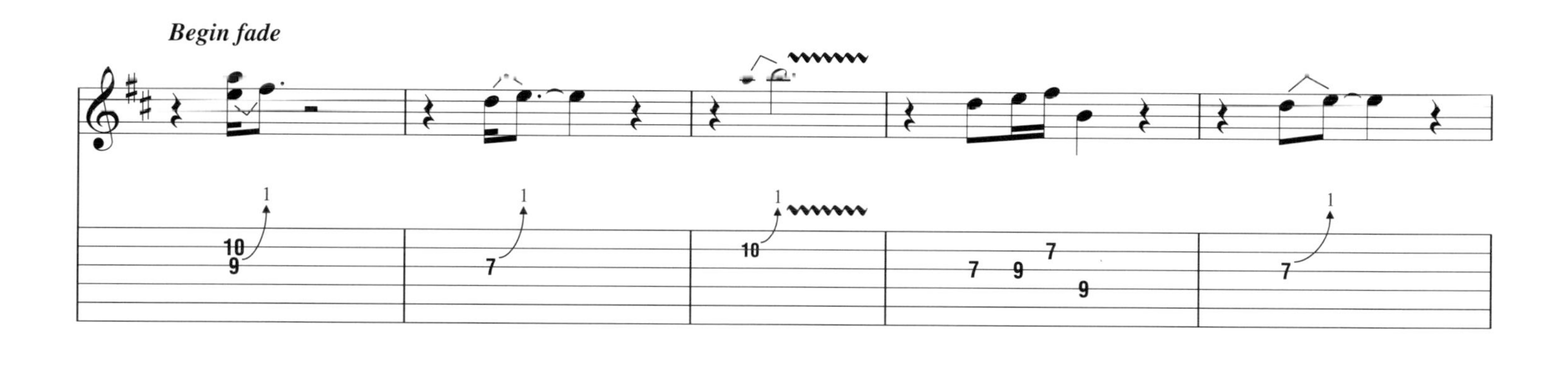

Fade out

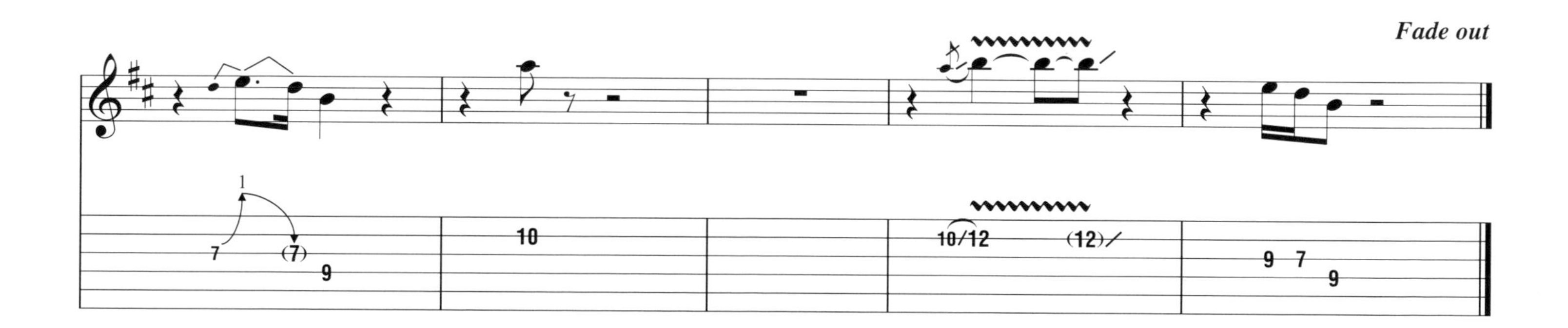

Additional Lyrics

3. The thrill is gone,
   It's gone away for good.
   Oh, the thrill is gone,
   Baby, it's gone away for good.
   Someday I know I'll be holdin' on, baby,
   Just like I know a good man should.

Guitar Notation Legend

THE MUSICAL STAFF shows pitches and rhythms and is divided by bar lines into measures. Pitches are named after the first seven letters of the alphabet.

TABLATURE graphically represents the guitar fingerboard. Each horizontal line represents a string, and each number represents a fret.

4th string, 2nd fret | 1st & 2nd strings open, played together | open D chord

HALF-STEP BEND: Strike the note and bend up 1/2 step.

WHOLE-STEP BEND: Strike the note and bend up one step.

GRACE NOTE BEND: Strike the note and bend up as indicated. The first note does not take up any time.

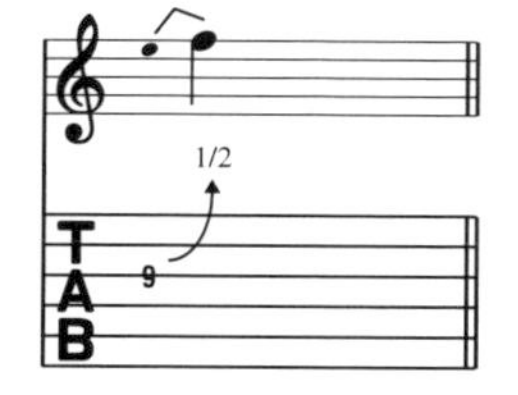

SLIGHT (MICROTONE) BEND: Strike the note and bend up 1/4 step.

BEND AND RELEASE: Strike the note and bend up as indicated, then release back to the original note. Only the first note is struck.

PRE-BEND: Bend the note as indicated, then strike it.

VIBRATO: The string is vibrated by rapidly bending and releasing the note with the fretting hand.

PALM MUTING: The note is partially muted by the pick hand lightly touching the string(s) just before the bridge.

HAMMER-ON: Strike the first (lower) note with one finger, then sound the higher note (on the same string) with another finger by fretting it without picking.

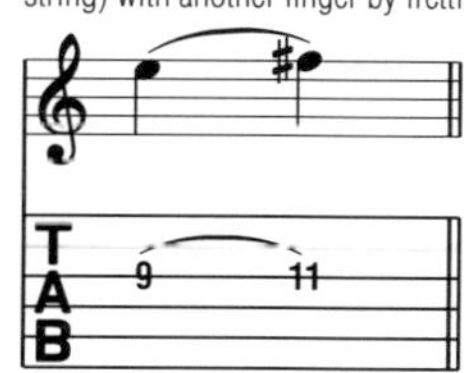

PULL-OFF: Place both fingers on the notes to be sounded. Strike the first note and without picking, pull the finger off to sound the second (lower) note.

LEGATO SLIDE: Strike the first note and then slide the same fret-hand finger up or down to the second note. The second note is not struck.

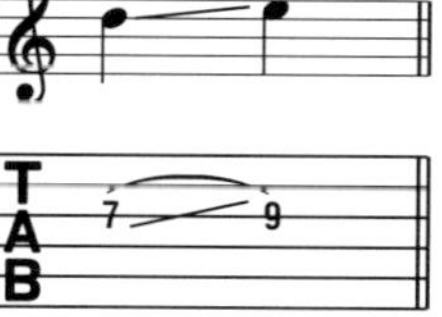

SHIFT SLIDE: Same as legato slide, except the second note is struck.

TRILL: Very rapidly alternate between the notes indicated by continuously hammering on and pulling off.

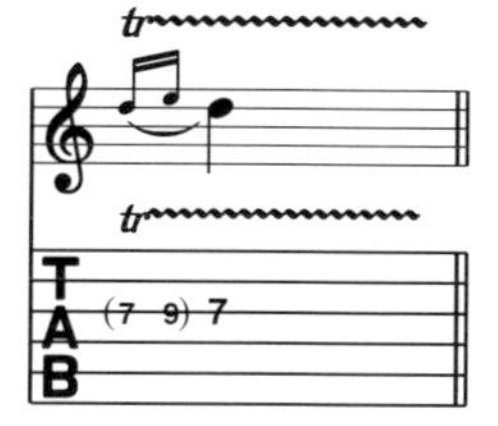

TAPPING: Hammer ("tap") the fret indicated with the pick-hand index or middle finger and pull off to the note fretted by the fret hand.

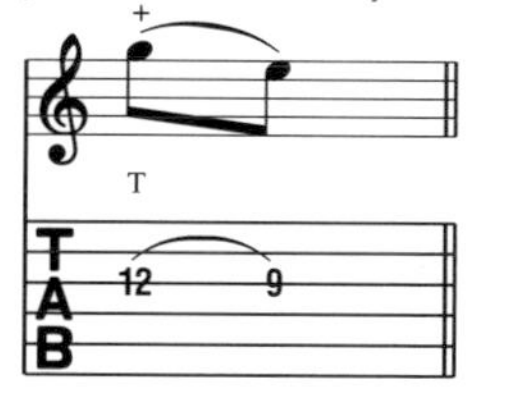

NATURAL HARMONIC: Strike the note while the fret-hand lightly touches the string directly over the fret indicated.

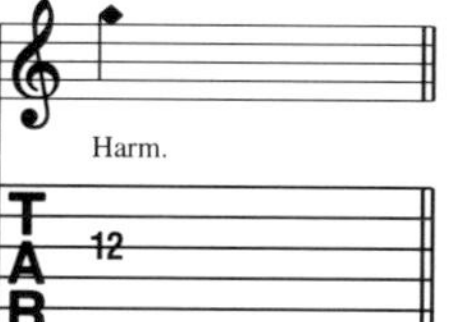

PINCH HARMONIC: The note is fretted normally and a harmonic is produced by adding the edge of the thumb or the tip of the index finger of the pick hand to the normal pick attack.

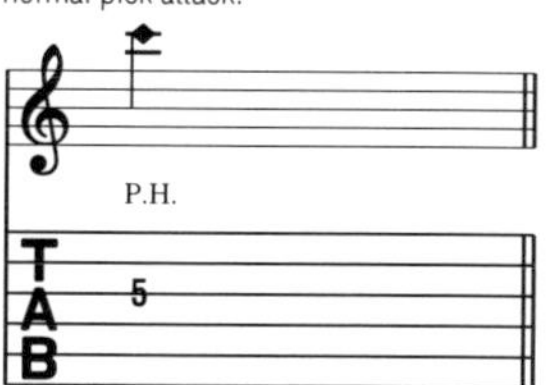

TREMOLO PICKING: The note is picked as rapidly and continuously as possible.

VIBRATO BAR DIVE AND RETURN: The pitch of the note or chord is dropped a specified number of steps (in rhythm) then returned to the original pitch.

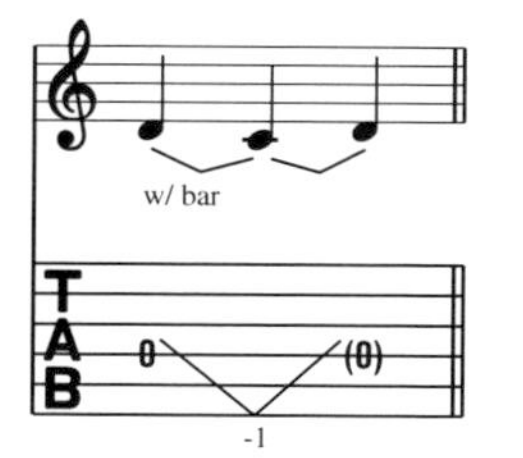

VIBRATO BAR SCOOP: Depress the bar just before striking the note, then quickly release the bar.

VIBRATO BAR DIP: Strike the note and then immediately drop a specified number of steps, then release back to the original pitch.

Additional Musical Definitions

(accent) • Accentuate note (play it louder)

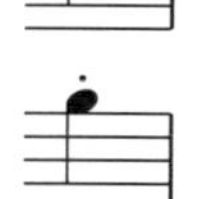

(staccato) • Play the note short

D.S. al Coda • Go back to the sign (𝄋), then play until the measure marked ***"To Coda"***, then skip to the section labelled ***"Coda."***

D.C. al Fine • Go back to the beginning of the song and play until the measure marked ***"Fine"*** (end).

Fill • Label used to identify a brief melodic figure which is to be inserted into the arrangement.

N.C. • Instrument is silent (drops out).

• Repeat measures between signs.

1. 2.

• When a repeated section has different endings, play the first ending only the first time and the second ending only the second time.

Complete song lists available online.

This series will help you play your favorite songs quickly and easily. Just follow the tab and listen to the audio to the hear how the guitar should sound, and then play along using the separate backing tracks. Audio files also include software to slow down the tempo without changing pitch. The melody and lyrics are included in the book so that you can sing or simply follow along.

INCLUDES TAB

VOL. 1 – ROCK .... 00699570 / $17.99
VOL. 2 – ACOUSTIC .... 00699569 / $17.99
VOL. 3 – HARD ROCK .... 00699573 / $19.99
VOL. 4 – POP/ROCK .... 00699571 / $16.99
VOL. 5 – THREE CHORD SONGS .... 00300985 / $16.99
VOL. 6 – '90S ROCK .... 00298615 / $16.99
VOL. 7 – BLUES .... 00699575 / $19.99
VOL. 8 – ROCK .... 00699585 / $16.99
VOL. 9 – EASY ACOUSTIC SONGS .... 00151708 / $16.99
VOL. 11 – EARLY ROCK .... 00699579 / $17.99
VOL. 12 – ROCK POP .... 00291724 / $17.99
VOL. 14 – BLUES ROCK .... 00699582 / $17.99
VOL. 15 – R&B .... 00699583 / $17.99
VOL. 16 – JAZZ .... 00699584 / $17.99
VOL. 17 – COUNTRY .... 00699588 / $17.99
VOL. 18 – ACOUSTIC ROCK .... 00699577 / $15.95
VOL. 20 – ROCKABILLY .... 00699580 / $17.99
VOL. 21 – SANTANA .... 00174525 / $19.99
VOL. 22 – CHRISTMAS .... 00699600 / $15.99
VOL. 23 – SURF .... 00699635 / $17.99
VOL. 24 – ERIC CLAPTON .... 00699649 / $19.99
VOL. 25 – THE BEATLES .... 00198265 / $19.99
VOL. 26 – ELVIS PRESLEY .... 00699643 / $17.99
VOL. 27 – DAVID LEE ROTH .... 00699645 / $16.95
VOL. 29 – BOB SEGER .... 00699647 / $16.99
VOL. 30 – KISS .... 00699644 / $17.99
VOL. 32 – THE OFFSPRING .... 00699653 / $14.95
VOL. 33 – ACOUSTIC CLASSICS .... 00699656 / $19.99
VOL. 35 – HAIR METAL .... 00699660 / $19.99
VOL. 36 – SOUTHERN ROCK .... 00699661 / $19.99
VOL. 37 – ACOUSTIC UNPLUGGED .... 00699662 / $22.99
VOL. 39 – '80s METAL .... 00699664 / $17.99
VOL. 40 – INCUBUS .... 00699668 / $17.95
VOL. 41 – ERIC CLAPTON .... 00699669 / $17.99
VOL. 42 – COVER BAND HITS .... 00211597 / $16.99
VOL. 43 – LYNYRD SKYNYRD .... 00699681 / $22.99
VOL. 44 – JAZZ GREATS .... 00699689 / $19.99
VOL. 45 – TV THEMES .... 00699718 / $14.95
VOL. 46 – MAINSTREAM ROCK .... 00699722 / $16.95
VOL. 47 – JIMI HENDRIX SMASH HITS .... 00699723 / $22.99
VOL. 48 – AEROSMITH CLASSICS .... 00699724 / $19.99
VOL. 49 – STEVIE RAY VAUGHAN .... 00699725 / $19.99
VOL. 50 – VAN HALEN: 1978-1984 .... 00110269 / $19.99
VOL. 51 – ALTERNATIVE '90s .... 00699727 / $14.99
VOL. 52 – FUNK .... 00699728 / $17.99
VOL. 53 – DISCO .... 00699729 / $14.99
VOL. 55 – POP METAL .... 00699731 / $14.95
VOL. 57 – GUNS 'N' ROSES .... 00159922 / $19.99
VOL. 59 – CHET ATKINS .... 00702347 / $22.99
VOL. 60 – 3 DOORS DOWN .... 00699774 / $14.95
VOL. 62 – CHRISTMAS CAROLS .... 00699798 / $12.95
VOL. 63 – CREEDENCE CLEARWATER REVIVAL .... 00699802 / $17.99
VOL. 64 – ULTIMATE OZZY OSBOURNE .... 00699803 / $22.99
VOL. 66 – THE ROLLING STONES .... 00699807 / $19.99
VOL. 67 – BLACK SABBATH .... 00699808 / $17.99
VOL. 68 – PINK FLOYD – DARK SIDE OF THE MOON .... 00699809 / $17.99
VOL. 71 – CHRISTIAN ROCK .... 00699824 / $14.95
VOL. 74 – SIMPLE STRUMMING SONGS .... 00151706 / $19.99
VOL. 75 – TOM PETTY .... 00699882 / $19.99
VOL. 76 – COUNTRY HITS .... 00699884 / $16.99
VOL. 77 – BLUEGRASS .... 00699910 / $17.99
VOL. 78 – NIRVANA .... 00700132 / $17.99
VOL. 79 – NEIL YOUNG .... 00700133 / $24.99
VOL. 81 – ROCK ANTHOLOGY .... 00700176 / $24.99
VOL. 82 – EASY ROCK SONGS .... 00700177 / $17.99
VOL. 83 – SUBLIME .... 00369114 / $17.99
VOL. 84 – STEELY DAN .... 00700200 / $19.99
VOL. 85 – THE POLICE .... 00700269 / $17.99
VOL. 86 – BOSTON .... 00700465 / $19.99
VOL. 87 – ACOUSTIC WOMEN .... 00700763 / $14.99
VOL. 88 – GRUNGE .... 00700467 / $16.99
VOL. 89 – REGGAE .... 00700468 / $15.99
VOL. 90 – CLASSICAL POP .... 00700469 / $14.99
VOL. 91 – BLUES INSTRUMENTALS .... 00700505 / $19.99
VOL. 92 – EARLY ROCK INSTRUMENTALS .... 00700506 / $17.99
VOL. 93 – ROCK INSTRUMENTALS .... 00700507 / $17.99
VOL. 94 – SLOW BLUES .... 00700508 / $16.99
VOL. 95 – BLUES CLASSICS .... 00700509 / $17.99
VOL. 96 – BEST COUNTRY HITS .... 00211615 / $16.99
VOL. 97 – CHRISTMAS CLASSICS .... 00236542 / $14.99
VOL. 99 – ZZ TOP .... 00700762 / $17.99
VOL. 100 – B.B. KING .... 00700466 / $17.99
VOL. 101 – SONGS FOR BEGINNERS .... 00701917 / $14.99
VOL. 102 – CLASSIC PUNK .... 00700769 / $14.99
VOL. 104 – DUANE ALLMAN .... 00700846 / $22.99
VOL. 105 – LATIN .... 00700939 / $16.99
VOL. 106 – WEEZER .... 00700958 / $17.99
VOL. 107 – CREAM .... 00701069 / $17.99
VOL. 108 – THE WHO .... 00701053 / $17.99
VOL. 109 – STEVE MILLER .... 00701054 / $19.99
VOL. 110 – SLIDE GUITAR HITS .... 00701055 / $17.99
VOL. 111 – JOHN MELLENCAMP .... 00701056 / $14.99
VOL. 112 – QUEEN .... 00701052 / $16.99
VOL. 113 – JIM CROCE .... 00701058 / $19.99
VOL. 114 – BON JOVI .... 00701060 / $17.99
VOL. 115 – JOHNNY CASH .... 00701070 / $17.99
VOL. 116 – THE VENTURES .... 00701124 / $17.99
VOL. 117 – BRAD PAISLEY .... 00701224 / $16.99
VOL. 118 – ERIC JOHNSON .... 00701353 / $19.99
VOL. 119 – AC/DC CLASSICS .... 00701356 / $19.99
VOL. 120 – PROGRESSIVE ROCK .... 00701457 / $14.99
VOL. 121 – U2 .... 00701508 / $17.99
VOL. 122 – CROSBY, STILLS & NASH .... 00701610 / $16.99
VOL. 123 – LENNON & McCARTNEY ACOUSTIC .... 00701614 / $16.99
VOL. 124 – SMOOTH JAZZ .... 00200664 / $17.99
VOL. 125 – JEFF BECK .... 00701687 / $19.99
VOL. 126 – BOB MARLEY .... 00701701 / $19.99
VOL. 127 – 1970s ROCK .... 00701739 / $17.99
VOL. 129 – MEGADETH .... 00701741 / $17.99
VOL. 130 – IRON MAIDEN .... 00701742 / $19.99
VOL. 131 – 1990s ROCK .... 00701743 / $14.99
VOL. 132 – COUNTRY ROCK .... 00701757 / $15.99
VOL. 133 – TAYLOR SWIFT .... 00701894 / $16.99
VOL. 135 – MINOR BLUES .... 00151350 / $17.99
VOL. 136 – GUITAR THEMES .... 00701922 / $14.99
VOL. 137 – IRISH TUNES .... 00701966 / $17.99
VOL. 138 – BLUEGRASS CLASSICS .... 00701967 / $17.99
VOL. 139 – GARY MOORE .... 00702370 / $19.99
VOL. 140 – MORE STEVIE RAY VAUGHAN .... 00702396 / $24.99
VOL. 141 – ACOUSTIC HITS .... 00702401 / $16.99
VOL. 142 – GEORGE HARRISON .... 00237697 / $17.99
VOL. 143 – SLASH .... 00702425 / $19.99
VOL. 144 – DJANGO REINHARDT .... 00702531 / $17.99
VOL. 145 – DEF LEPPARD .... 00702532 / $19.99
VOL. 146 – ROBERT JOHNSON .... 00702533 / $16.99
VOL. 147 – SIMON & GARFUNKEL .... 14041591 / $19.99
VOL. 148 – BOB DYLAN .... 14041592 / $17.99
VOL. 149 – AC/DC HITS .... 14041593 / $19.99
VOL. 150 – ZAKK WYLDE .... 02501717 / $19.99
VOL. 151 – J.S. BACH .... 02501730 / $16.99
VOL. 152 – JOE BONAMASSA .... 02501751 / $24.99
VOL. 153 – RED HOT CHILI PEPPERS .... 00702990 / $22.99
VOL. 155 – ERIC CLAPTON UNPLUGGED .... 00703085 / $19.99
VOL. 156 – SLAYER .... 00703770 / $19.99
VOL. 157 – FLEETWOOD MAC .... 00101382 / $17.99
VOL. 159 – WES MONTGOMERY .... 00102593 / $22.99
VOL. 160 – T-BONE WALKER 00102641/ $17.99
VOL. 161 – THE EAGLES ACOUSTIC .... 00102659 / $19.99
VOL. 162 – THE EAGLES HITS .... 00102667 / $19.99
VOL. 163 – PANTERA .... 00103036 / $19.99
VOL. 164 – VAN HALEN: 1986-1995 .... 00110270 / $19.99
VOL. 165 – GREEN DAY .... 00210343 / $17.99
VOL. 166 – MODERN BLUES .... 00700764 / $16.99
VOL. 167 – DREAM THEATER .... 00111938 / $24.99
VOL. 168 – KISS .... 00113421 / $17.99
VOL. 170 – THREE DAYS GRACE .... 00117337 / $16.99
VOL. 171 – JAMES BROWN .... 00117420 / $16.99
VOL. 172 – THE DOOBIE BROTHERS .... 00119670 / $17.99
VOL. 173 – TRANS-SIBERIAN ORCHESTRA .... 00119907 / $19.99
VOL. 174 – SCORPIONS .... 00122119 / $19.99
VOL. 175 – MICHAEL SCHENKER .... 00122127 / $19.99
VOL. 176 – BLUES BREAKERS WITH JOHN MAYALL & ERIC CLAPTON .... 00122132 / $19.99
VOL. 177 – ALBERT KING .... 00123271 / $17.99
VOL. 178 – JASON MRAZ .... 00124165 / $17.99
VOL. 179 – RAMONES .... 00127073 / $17.99
VOL. 180 – BRUNO MARS .... 00129706 / $16.99
VOL. 181 – JACK JOHNSON .... 00129854 / $16.99
VOL. 182 – SOUNDGARDEN .... 00138161 / $17.99
VOL. 183 – BUDDY GUY .... 00138240 / $17.99
VOL. 184 – KENNY WAYNE SHEPHERD .... 00138258 / $17.99
VOL. 185 – JOE SATRIANI .... 00139457 / $19.99
VOL. 186 – GRATEFUL DEAD .... 00139459 / $17.99
VOL. 187 – JOHN DENVER .... 00140839 / $19.99
VOL. 188 – MÖTLEY CRÜE .... 00141145 / $19.99
VOL. 189 – JOHN MAYER .... 00144350 / $22.99
VOL. 190 – DEEP PURPLE .... 00146152 / $19.99
VOL. 191 – PINK FLOYD CLASSICS .... 00146164 / $17.99
VOL. 192 – JUDAS PRIEST .... 00151352 / $19.99
VOL. 193 – STEVE VAI .... 00156028 / $19.99
VOL. 195 – METALLICA: 1983-1988 .... 00234291 / $24.99
VOL. 196 – METALLICA: 1991-2016 .... 00234292 / $22.99

Prices, contents, and availability subject to change without notice.

www.halleonard.com